GOSPEL BASICS

PS. 40

GOSPEL BASICS

Trusting, Following, and Winning Christ

Andrew A. Bonar

THE BANNER OF TRUTH TRUST

THE BANNER OF TRUTH TRUST

3 Murrayfield Road, Edinburgh EH12 6EL, UK
P.O. Box 621, Carlisle, PA 17013, USA

First published in 1878 as *Gospel Truths*
This rearranged and reset edition
© The Banner of Truth Trust 2011

ISBN: 978 1 84871 123 5

Typeset in 11/15 pt Adobe Caslon Pro at
The Banner of Truth Trust

Printed in the U.S.A. by
Versa Press, Inc.,
East Peoria, IL

CONTENTS

There is always life and sweetness about the writings of Andrew A. Bonar. These papers upon various subjects are quite new to us, though they appear to have been published before in various forms. We have exceedingly much enjoyed reading several of the chapters, and we do our readers a service when we commend 'Gospel Truths' to their notice. Striking but not sensational, spiritual but not maudlin, the style and matter are altogether to our mind.

C. H. Spurgeon
The Sword and the Trowel,
March, 1879

PREFACE

This volume is a collection of pieces written at different times, and generally with a view to special circumstances. Thus 'Angel Workers' was originally given at a meeting of Workers, who afterwards asked to have it in print. 'What Gives Assurance' was found useful at the time of an Awakening at Ferryden, in the year 1859. Each piece has had a history of its own, and all are brought together in this form at the suggestion of friends.[1]

A. A. B.

Glasgow, 1878.

[1] The present publisher has altered the form of the original by re-arranging the chapters of this new edition into a more logical order. D. M. McIntyre's piece on Bonar's preaching has also been added.

DR ANDREW BONAR
AS A PREACHER

It will not seem to be partiality on the part of any who were accustomed to wait on Dr Bonar's ministry, that they should rank him high among the preachers of his age. He himself would not have admitted the correctness of this view: I do not think that he would even have wished that this should be thought of him. His preaching seemed to be singularly effortless. The truth entrusted to him held him in possession, and he had no apparent carefulness regarding the mode of its presentation. God had spoken to him; it was his care to transmit in its simplicity and integrity the message which he bore. But the very consciousness that he was 'the Lord's messenger in the Lord's message' gave a peculiar authority to his words, and clothed them with an impressiveness which was sometimes indescribable. There was a remarkable power of *revelation* in his pulpit utterances. He moved serenely among things unseen; it was evident that they were visible to himself, and so at times they broke into light, and shone full on the soul of the hearer. Prayer is sometimes offered for a preacher that he may be concealed behind his message. One has seldom seen this desirable effect more perfectly produced than in the case of Dr Andrew A. Bonar. He stood between the living and the dead, conscious at once of the ravages of the plague and of the healing power of the gospel committed to him, but he himself was hidden within the shadow of God's hand.

Yet if one had freedom of mind to exercise a critical judgment on preaching which stirred and met the deepest cravings of the heart, and which seemed at times to be little more than a diaphanous veil between the hearer and the Divine Presence, it would be found that it satisfied the highest requirements of the preacher's art. The language was simple, but of spotless purity: every word was well-born, and demeaned itself with dignity. Although there were no rhetorical effects, there was at times a soaring imagination, and very frequently a strain of the loftiest poetry. If Dr Bonar had not been a preacher by the grace of God, he might have been a literary critic by the gifts of nature. He was a master of our strong, sweet English tongue. Precision of thought was fitly wedded to his limpid speech. In the conventional sense of the term, Dr Bonar prepared no 'great' sermons. He did not try to rise by a distinct literary effort to an outstanding occasion. But among his own people he walked invariably on his 'high places', and sometimes he took to himself the wings of the morning, and soared through the blue heavens towards the throne of the Eternal.

When I heard him first he was already aged, but his natural force was not abated. I can see him still, the kindly face crowned with silver hair, a face bright with the thought of God, but grave with the cast at eternity. I still seem to hear his high-pitched, musical voice, with a world of tenderness in its tones. Never have I seen a fairer embodiment of Bunyan's portrait of the Supreme Evangelist: 'It had eyes lifted up to heaven, the best of books in his hand, the law of truth was written upon his lips, the world was behind his back; it stood as if it pleaded with men, and a crown of gold did hang over its head.'

Dr Bonar's preaching was invariably expository. At the service which commemorated his ministerial jubilee he said, with his accustomed modesty: 'You know I never aspired to be an intellectual preacher. Nor did I try to be eloquent; it was not in my power. I sought to be a Bible expositor, to stand at the well, and roll off the stone, and water the flocks, and send them away; always looking to the Chief Shepherd, and the day when he shall appear and tell his approval of work done for him.' For the interpretation of Scripture few have been as richly endowed as Dr Bonar. He had a powerful, yet keen and nimble, mind, a fine literary sense, an admirable critical faculty, wide and penetrating scholarship, and a passionate love for the Word of God. I scarcely think that there was a single verse of the Old Testament or of the New which he had not subjected to an examination under the microscope. He was perfectly at home in the original languages of Scripture, and he was acquainted, as very few have been, with the course of interpretation. The most unlettered person in his congregation would be sensible of the simple directness of his terse comments, but comparatively few knew the wealth of learning out of which those luminous sentences came, or realised the cost by which this clearness was won. At the beginning of their respective ministries, Robert Murray M'Cheyne cautioned Andrew Bonar against what seemed to the former a habit of obscurity. We may suppose, therefore, that Dr Bonar's luminosity of speech was not so much the gift of a transparent nature as the gain of a cultured mind. Yet nature, undoubtedly, added her part. His Hebrew professor, 'Rabbi' Duncan, was accustomed to follow out a long train of excogitation—'theologizing' he called it—and then condense all his laborious thinking into an aphorism. Dr Bonar also was a 'master of sentences'; he could convey in a perfectly lucid phrase, compact and memorable, the deepest experience, the profoundest thought. But that pregnant utterance was not always the painful result of close thinking, it was frequently the fruit of open vision, for there was more than scholarship in his expositions—there was insight. He was one of those rare souls, rare in any age, who possess a balanced genius. Like the beloved disciple, whom in many ways he much resembled, he was both a reasoner and a seer, and it would be hard to say whether the seeing faculty or the discursive predominated. This combination, the force of his understanding and the reach of his vision, fitted him in quite a remarkable degree for his great life-work of displaying the hidden things of God. But it is time to turn to the subject matter of Dr Bonar's preaching.

It is a fixed law of the spirit that no man can utter with perfect conviction that which has not been realised at least in part in his own experience. The life of a minister is the power of his ministrations. Now the cardinal experience of any great preacher is his conversion to God.

As we open the volume in which Dr Bonar's private diary has been preserved, we are at once made aware that a prolonged conflict between grace and nature is drawing near to a happy termination. The field of this conflict is a mind singularly rich in native quality, a heart strong and gentle, a life outwardly without blemish. Several stages in this victory of grace are depicted in faint outline. Each of these seems to offer a fresh illustration of the fact to which we have just alluded, that a man's preaching inevitably flows through those channels which grace carves out in his personal experience.

At the age of eighteen, after having heard a sermon preached by a ministerial friend, the young student writes: 'I came home in deep anxiety to be saved, and I was, I trust, enabled to choose Christ for my Saviour, depending upon the Holy Spirit's assistance to keep me. But still I fear and tremble lest all be not well.' It is apparent that God had already spoken the creative word, and that the light of his glory had been seen in the face of Jesus Christ. But morning clouds and mists of dew obscured for a time the brightness of that sun. The sentence which follows strikes one clear note of Dr Bonar's preaching: 'Hearing Mr Buchanan, of Leith, who showed me I was resting my hope upon my belief, not upon the Object of that belief.' A few weeks later he adds: 'I sometimes think God is thus dealing with me that I may afterwards be better fitted to teach others.' As all who have listened to Andrew Bonar's preaching are aware, his unfailing insistence on Christ as the object of faith was one of its most impressive characteristics.

About this time a sermon by Edward Irving on the parable of the sower cast into the young inquirer's soul 'some of the first beams of light' with regard to spiritual truth. The substance of that sermon has no doubt been preserved in the author's treatise on that parable. With singular force of language the great preacher tracks to their last place of concealment the deceits and hypocrisies of the human heart. The impression made on Andrew Bonar's awakened mind by this searching discourse may have added to the keenness of his natural power of discrimination, and have fitted him to estimate at their just value the sometimes dubious evidences of grace displayed in the lives of those with whom he came in contact.

But it was when he was reading the great evangelical classic, William Guthrie of Fenwick, that the seal of assurance was impressed upon his heart. 'In reading Guthrie's *Saving Interest* I have been led to hope that I may be in Christ, though I have never known it.' All the marks of faith which that experienced writer sets forth as the proof of grace were recognisable to the anxious search of the young disciple. From that hour it can hardly be said that he ever doubted. Recalling this very episode, he said in the early days of his Glasgow ministry, 'For more than thirty years . . . I have never been shaken in my quiet resting on the Lord Jesus.' And shortly before his death he looked back to that never-to-be-forgotten hour, and testified that from that time he had not on one day, during more than sixty years, missed his way to the Mercy Seat.

We are able, I think, to turn to the very page from which the light of God streamed out on the dark pathway of this already deeply exercised soul. Guthrie is speaking of the properties of faith. Faith, he says, must be personal, cordial, rational, resolute.

Personal: 'A man himself, and in his own proper person, must close with Christ Jesus.'

Cordial: 'There must be in believing a . . . kindly love, so well-grounded and deeply engaging that many waters cannot quench it.'

Rational: 'I mean . . . that a man be in calmness of spirit, and, as it were, in his cold blood, in closing with Christ Jesus; not in a single fit of affection, which soon vanisheth.'

Resolute: 'The man whose heart is a-laying out for Christ Jesus cannot say, "There is a lion in the street." If he cannot have access by the door, he will break through the roof of the house.'

From the opening of his ministry to its close, during more than half a century, Dr Bonar, in the strictest and yet the fullest sense of the term, preached Christ.

Theology has always endeavoured to form its system round the person of Christ, but it has been forced again and again to register defeat. One governing conception after another impresses the minds of men, and various doctrinal schemes are formulated with unifying centres. But faith points unshakenly Christ-wards, and all preaching which is vital brings its hearers into the presence of the Incarnate Word. *The Gospel Pointing to the Person of Christ* is the title of one of Dr Bonar's most useful works, and it fitly describes the bent of his preaching. The deepest element in this persistent presentation of Christ to men was, undoubtedly, his continual remembrance of what the Lord had done for himself. 'Little as I am acquainted with the Lord', he says, 'I will leave it as my testimony that there is none like him. God has been good to a soul that but poorly sought him. Often on Sabbath evenings I have felt, "Whom have I in heaven but thee? and there is none upon earth whom I desire beside thee."' Christ's actual presence with him was the sunshine of his life, and as the years passed that radiance brightened along his path. 'The Lord has given me all Christ, an incomparably great gift, and I have not understood it all these many years. The Lord has not given me a heart to perceive, nor eyes to see, unto this day.'

But Christ is also the sum of the Divine revelation: 'To him give all the prophets witness.' And, with no fanciful exegesis, but in accordance with the most exact principles of interpretation, Dr Bonar found in every page of the written Word some delineation of his Lord. A ministerial friend said jestingly to him once: 'I think, Andrew, that you belong to the Old Dispensation.' It was not so; no one lived more unchangingly beneath the opened heavens of the Pentecostal age; but he had found in Christ the harmony of the two covenants. His commentaries on Leviticus and the Psalms are full of Christ, but it is Christ foreseen and waited for. The deepest impression which the former volume leaves on one's mind is the holiness of God; what the latter work brings most vividly to one's imagination and remembrance is the voluntariness of the Redeemer's sacrifice. The Aaronic tabernacle was in his view a richly stored gallery of gospel images. To him, as to the apocalyptic angel, the testimony of Jesus was the spirit of prophecy, and Old Testament history the record of 'the evangelic preparation' for Christ. 'Every line in this inspired Bible', he would say, 'is wet with the dew of the Spirit's love.'

It was, however, his consuming desire for the salvation of his people that held his preaching so closely to the person of Christ. Those of his hearers who had been perplexed by some doctrinal subtlety found their doubts resolved when they were brought face to face with him who is the sole object of faith. 'Leave self and sight', he said to such, 'everything and every person, but Christ alone.' I do not know that he ever preached a sermon in which he did not clearly and with more or less particularity set forth Christ crucified and risen, as the Redeemer whose blood avails for sin, whose Spirit gives life to a death-bound soul. And yet, just because his preaching was so exactly scriptural, there was a perpetual freshness in his enforcement of the familiar themes. On the morning on which his Glasgow ministry was to open, he prayed, 'Lord, let there be the print of thy footsteps upon the floor of our church today.' His first text in Finnieston was Proverbs 11:30: 'He that winneth souls is wise.' He began his sermon with these words: 'It is my heart's desire and prayer that my ministry here may be a proclamation of the heart and ways of our compassionate God to mankind-sinners, and that I may proclaim his heart and ways in the mind of Christ.'

The phrase, 'mankind-sinners', reminds us of the fact that from the opening of his ministry he had been much impressed by what is still known in Scotland as 'Marrow Theology'. *The Marrow of Modern Divinity*, a catena of quotations from the writings of the Reformers and the best divines of the succeeding age, compiled by a godly bookseller who was an untitled member of a Presbyterian Church in London, and published by Giles Calvert in 1645, did much to recall the preaching of the eighteenth century from the somewhat formal statements regarding the operation of grace which had become common, to the freer and more scriptural expressions which characterized the great documents of the Reformation. Of the significant phrases which lifted this book into something like notoriety, one of the most suggestive was that sentence of Ezekiel Culverwells, in which he asserts that God gave Christ as 'a grant or deed of gift to mankind sinners'. When Dr Bonar began his ministry in Collace he became aware of a general impression that (to use his own words) 'some of us who are so much together are considered by ministers as making a new school of preaching'. I think that the distinction observed may have been chiefly in relation to this matter. The unrestrained offer of Christ to sinners of mankind was one notable mark of Dr Bonar's preaching. 'Be done looking at your faith. Look at the object of your faith, and your rest has begun.' 'We stand at Calvary, and hear Christ say "It is finished!" We say, "Amen", and lift the cup of life to our lips.' 'A sinner', he often repeated, 'so long as he is unpardoned has a right to only one thing in the universe—only one—and that is the blood of the Lord Jesus Christ.'

The Cross of Christ, as one would naturally conclude from what has been said, was the continually recurring theme of Dr Bonar's preaching. In the *Reminiscences* we are informed that it was 'his oft-repeated desire for himself that he might never to the day of his death preach to his people, or be with them in any of their meetings, without saying something about what gives peace to the sinner.' His prayer one day in his own church was, 'Lord, never let anyone occupy this pulpit who does not preach Christ and him crucified.' It was the finished work of the Redeemer which he held forth as the sinner's only ground of confidence: 'Look at the price Christ paid in working out your redemption, and then return and lay your weary head on the bosom of God, with the ransom-money in your hand.' There are indications not to be distrusted that the current of theological thought is flowing strongly in the direction of a revived interest in the meaning of the death of Christ. And yet, one does not often find in contemporary literature that particular emphasis which so remarkably characterized Dr Bonar's preaching of the Cross. It was as if he looked down from the summits of the Divine righteousness, and saw with God the burning and spotless holiness which distinguished the atoning sacrifice. He bent down with reverence to look into those things which interpret and transfigure the Cross. He stood within the Presence of God: and in that pure light he saw light. His preaching of the Cross was always warm with personal application. He viewed the death of Christ with such feelings of adoring love as may stir the hearts of the glorified who dwell for ever under and around the throne where the Lamb has his seat. 'Suppose that I, a sinner, be walking along yon golden street, passing by one angel after another. I can hear them say as I pass through their ranks, "A sinner! a crimson sinner!" Should my feet totter? Should my eye grow dim? No; I can say to them, "Yes, a sinner; a crimson sinner; but a sinner brought near by a forsaken Saviour, and now a sinner who has boldness to enter into the Holiest through the blood of Christ."'

Dr Bonar dwelt with remarkable fullness on the believer's union with Christ. John Bunyan acknowledges with regard to himself that it was late in his ministry when the Lord showed him 'something of the mystery of union with Christ.' But with Dr Bonar this was a copious source of exhortation from the first. Here again his preaching was distilled out of his own experience. His personal longings after holiness gave a marvellous power to his presentation of the fullness of Christ. He himself sighed for God as the hunted stag pants for the waterbrooks, and the intensity of his ardour quickened the zeal of many. It was this in part which made the communion times in Finnieston to be seasons of such peculiar solemnity. Of one of these days of the unveiling of the face of God he says: 'Yesterday I felt a little of abounding grace, and the blessedness of being sure yet to be holy, holy, holy. It seemed a very short day; the sun hasted to go down, I thought. We would need a long eternity, or heaven would be no heaven, it would be so soon over.'

That sanctification is by faith, and that it is the believer's duty and privilege to dedicate himself wholly to the Lord, seemed to the older Scottish theologians to be implied in the very fact of conversion. It was from this point that Dr Bonar's life in Christ proceeded. From the beginning he confessed that he was not his own, and he counted all things but loss for the excellency of the knowledge of Christ Jesus his Lord. The holy enterprise and 'endurance with joyfulness' which marked his heavenward life gave edge and glow to his preaching, till it sometimes seemed to be as a sword of flame.

The shadow which in a world of sin attends holiness, and which broods within the name of God itself, became visible as he spoke. With a solemn awe upon his spirit he pleaded with men to be reconciled to God, and warned them of the day of wrath. There are some alive today who will never forget his utterance of warnings in which a pathetic tenderness mingled with the dread solemnities of eternity. 'I think that the shower of fire and brimstone was wet with the tears of God as it fell, for God has "no pleasure in the death of him that dieth".'

Dr Bonar's preaching was pre-eminently practical. The superficial distinction between an evangelistic and ethical gospel had no place in his scheme of thought. He faithfully obeyed the injunction of Paul the Apostle: 'These things I will that thou affirm constantly, that they which have believed in God might be careful to maintain good works.' With patient exactness he laid the burden of Christian obligation on the hearts of his hearers. In consequence of this practical direction in his preaching, his words went home to the consciences of his people, sometimes in a strange and arresting way. Again and again a hearer would be startled to find that his secret thoughts were made the theme of pulpit discourse. One who had observed this fact asked him for an explanation. He replied quaintly, 'It is not strange. You know I am just Balaam's ass, and the words are given. The Spirit knows what you all need.'

It would not be right to omit mention of the fact that Dr Bonar's preaching was pervaded with the spirit of gladness. This characteristic was the fruit of grace rather than the outcome of nature. He rejoiced in God with a joy which was full of glory. And he never failed to persuade his people to the realisation of this holy gladness. 'True godliness', he said, 'is just joy in God.' And again, 'A believer's life should be like a long, happy day, spent in the sunshine of God's face.' He dwelt much on the jubilant felicity of the Psalter, and the grave but triumphant confidence of the ancient saints. He would often insist that God is the gladness of our joy, that fellowship with him contains the essence of all blessedness. He constantly re-affirmed the law of the apostolic church—'Rejoice evermore.' Over and over again he reminded his hearers that joy was the gift of the dying Lord. 'Do not refuse joy from the Man of Sorrows', he would say, 'He gained it by his suffering.'

Much of this holy gladness flowed from the thought of our Lord's return. In his student-days Dr Bonar attended Edward Irving's Edinburgh lectures, and he notes in his diary, even before the 'great change' had been realised in his experience: 'Have been hearing Mr Irving's lectures all the week, and am persuaded now that his views of the coming Christ are truth.' The main point of Dr Bonar's prophetical system was the premillennial advent of the Lord. He did not presume to determine times and seasons, but he was disposed to think that the accomplishment of the 'blessed hope' was drawing near. He thought it possible that some of those who heard him might be 'alive and remain' at the appearing of the Bridegroom. He found in practice that a habitual outlook towards the Lord's return fostered a spirit of preparedness to meet the Coming One, and so became a potent aid to sanctification. But perhaps it was his love to the Master more than any other consideration which made this doctrine so dear to him. He used to tell, with much enjoyment, an incident related in Wodrow's Analecta of a Dr Bonar, minister in Maybole in the seventeenth century—presumably an ancestor of his own. A number of ministers had come together, and the conversation turned to the advent of Christ. There were some who thought that he might come before the Millennium, others that he would not come till afterwards. This aged man sat in silence, listening; presently they appealed to him: 'Father Bonar', they said, 'what do you think about this?' He replied that he had not given attention to that particular point, and added: 'If I live till our Lord Jesus come, this one thing I know, that I shall make him as welcome as any of you all.' This incident perfectly describes Dr Bonar's own attitude: his daily response to this great gospel promise was, 'Even so, come, Lord Jesus.'

In this very imperfect remembrance of Dr Bonar's preaching I have not been able adequately to emphasise one of its main features: I mean, his earnestness in pointing sinners to the Lamb of God. With Samuel Rutherford he might have said, regarding his unsaved people, that they were his tears by night, his sighs by day. He thirsted for their salvation. Their heaven, he said, would be to him two heavens. He brought his ministry in Collace to a close with these words: 'I beseech you, receive Christ today. I beseech you by the remembrance of past Sabbaths, by the many witnesses that the Lord sent among you from time to time, by the messages of grace so many and so varied, by the joy that your salvation would give above as well as here and to yourselves, by the thought of approaching death, by the thought of the Lord's speedy coming, by the opening of yonder veil, when eternity shall receive you and time be for ever gone—receive Christ now.'

To his people of Finnieston he uttered no farewell. He was busied to the last in pastoral duty. Then 'God's finger touched him, and he slept.'

D. M. McIntyre

I

DREAMS GONE;
DESOLATIONS COME

As a dream when one awaketh; so, O Lord, when thou awakest,
thou shalt despise their image.
Psalm 73:20

'You may go to hell asleep; but you cannot go to heaven asleep', says one who mourned over the deep delusion of unconverted men. The river Niagara flows on very smoothly, though swiftly, when it is near the cataract; it is perhaps nowhere so smooth as just before plunging over the rocks. Often, often is it thus with the sinner's life and end. No summer day was ever fairer, yet no night ever came on so sudden and so dark. 'Wherefore do the wicked live, become old, yea, are mighty in power? Their houses are safe from fear, neither is the rod of God upon them. They send forth their little ones like a flock, and their children dance. They take the timbrel and harp, and rejoice at the sound of the organ. They spend their days in wealth, and *in a moment go down to the grave*' (*Job* 21:7-13). Theirs has been a life with little care and much mirth. But sickness comes; fever is on them, and companions keep aloof; then come stupor, restlessness, death! Where is the soul? 'Oh, *he was well resigned!*' says some one, afraid lest the possibility of being lost should even be hinted at. But what was the foundation of this resignation,—this supposed peace? What if this peace was only

1

the sultry calm before the thunder? Was it not conscience asleep? For many die thus, and have a terrible awakening. The Word of God has said of such men, 'How are they brought into desolation as in a moment! They are utterly consumed with terrors. As a dream when one awaketh' (*Psa.* 73:19-20). Life's dreams are over; the stern reality has come.

1. *Their dreams are over.* God has awoke them, and they cast their eyes around. Where are they now? That lurid gleam is not the dawn! These forms are not friends! They essay to go forth, but it is in vain; they are like Samson when his strength was gone. They have come to that time of which it is written, 'He died, and was buried; and in hell he lifted up his eyes' (*Luke* 16:22-23).

They used to have their *dreams about an Eternal World.* They thought all said about it was mere words. This present world was all. But now they see too surely that there is another world; it was that this present world was an unreal one, and has melted away as snow. They are in a world where there is nothing of earth; none of its pursuits, none of its business, none of its sport, or mirth, or pleasure. No streets, no markets, no cities here! There is no sleep here; no time marked by hours; no bell to announce morn or even. 'Time shall be no more.' Earth is over. Like Napoleon at St Helena, when from the rocky height he looked out on boundless ocean,—no armies now, no marshals to receive command, no kings or kingdoms here. O poor soul! 'The fashion of the world has passed away.'

They used to have their *dreams about Sin.* They fancied it was a fiction, nothing real. Stolen waters were sweet, and forbidden fruit to be desired. But the dream is over. They see that sin is awfully real! The smallest sin has in it the sentence: 'Thou shalt die.' Every sin appears now a mighty mountain overhanging the soul, crushing out of it all hope, and overwhelming it with curse and wrath. They see, they feel the sting of sin; it has begun to inflict the wounds which none can ever heal. 'The wages of sin is death' (*Rom.* 6:23). What a meaning there is in that saying now! That death is no dream.

They used to have their *dreams about Hell.* They said it was nowhere; they scoffingly proclaimed that the idea of it was only a device of some who wished to terrify their fellows. They were sure that God had never kindled any such fire, and would never doom any soul to any such prison. But they have been rudely awakened out of their dream. They see hell now. There it is, stretching out on every side. They will never forget the gates shut upon them as they entered, precluding every hope of escape. O dreadful darkness! tormenting devils! unfeeling company! Now and then, it may be, some of the lost cry one to the other, 'How long?'; and one to the other utters the terrible response, 'For ever and for ever!' They find now there is a real hell, and that it has everlasting pains, and thirst such as a man sometimes felt on earth when he would have given kingdoms for one drop of water; and above all, that it has remorse, and fear, and every form of misery, ceaselessly sweeping through their soul, as the wild winds used to do over earth's sea when it could not rest. Christ's threefold utterance is true, 'Their worm dieth not, and the fire is not quenched' (*Mark* 9:44, 46, 48). The infinite God in very truth has poured out vials of wrath on sinners.

They used to have their *dreams about God.* They were sure it would be found that God was too merciful to send even one soul into misery. They were sure he was not what some few people asserted that the Bible said he was, a God who punished every violation of his holy law, and insisted on satisfaction being found by the sinner ere he would receive him into heaven. But they have been, alas! suddenly awakened out of this dream, and lo! yonder is the Judge, and the Great White Throne on which they read the writing, 'Holy, holy, holy, is the Lord.' 'He will by no means clear the guilty.' Ah! they find God was speaking only the truth when he sent messengers to tell them, that 'into his presence should enter nothing that defileth.'They find he keeps to that solemn word spoken to the sinner on earth about Jesus; 'He that believeth shall be saved, and he that believeth not shall be damned.'

Yes! *as a dream 'when one awaketh'!* There *is* another world. There *is* reality in sin. There *is* an eternal hell. God is not only loving and gracious, but just, holy, and true to his word. It is said that once, somewhere in the Mediterranean, many years ago, a captain with his ship had come upon a sunken rock, and barely escaped. On coming home, he told the Admiralty of his discovery, and had the spot put down in the chart: but one present scoffed at the discovery as a mere imagination, and declared that he would ere long sail his vessel over that fictitious rock! In order to carry his boast into action, he did set sail, and coming near the spot, with the chart spread out, called the ship's company to stand with him and be witnesses of his exposure of the delusion. In a quarter of an hour they would be on the rock, if it existed: so the captain stood with watch in hand, and when at last the fifteen minutes had passed, shouted out, 'I told you it was a mere dream; we have passed the spot, and there is nothing!' But scarcely had he uttered the words, when a harsh, grating sound was heard, and the vessel struck; the keel had grazed the rock; *the rock was there;* it was no dream! Pale with vexation, and unable to face the men who had heard his vain boasting, he leapt into the sea, and buried his shame in the waves. Even thus, deluded soul, shall thy vain fancies be dispelled. 'How are they brought into desolation as in a moment! they are utterly consumed with terrors! *as a dream when one awaketh.'* The words of God are no dream.

2. *Their desolation has come.* They are stripped of everything they ever enjoyed, everything of earth; as with us, one carried to prison is carefully stripped of his dress, and of all that was his. It is in all respects utter 'desolation'. No rest is left for them, for 'they rest not

day nor night', while 'the weary' (the believer who was so often made wearied by their ways) has entered on his eternal Sabbath. In vain do partial friends say at his grave, 'He is at his rest'; the lost soul has been stripped of it all for ever.

They are beyond conception lonely and 'desolate'. No companionship there furnishes relief to that awful solitude; the five brethren of the rich man (*Luke* 16:28), when they come to join him, are like fuel flung on the fire. No one there breathes sympathy; no one speaks of pity! no advocate pleads even once on their behalf. They risked all, and have lost all.

Think of one doomed to perpetual imprisonment, thrust down into the deep, dark dungeon of some great fortress, and left to die and rot there, forsaken and forgotten. At times, the man may hear overhead the sound of happy voices, and unmistakable intimation that others are enjoying light and life to the full. All this, by contrast, just adds to the intensity of his insupportable loneliness. He has been dropped out of the memory of his fellow-men. But all this is a mere hint of the inconceivable midnight of gloom and lonely desolation wrapped up in the terrible words of the prophet Jeremiah (23:39), when telling us that the Judge declares, 'Behold I, even I, *will utterly forget you!*' They are left in the prison that shall never be opened,—left alone, unnoticed for ever, uncared for, *forgotten by God!* Surely this is *'desolation'*. Heaven and hope are out of sight for ever, for even God refuses now to bestow one thought upon the sentenced soul.

'O that men were wise, that they would understand this, and consider their latter end' (*Deut.* 32:29). At any rate, shall God's children not act like men awake, who see others asleep on the slope of a precipice? Men of God, do you not care whether or not these dreamers sleep on? A word from you might be blessed to arouse them, and break in upon their dreams. If you have reason to fear that some whom you once knew are already lost, all the more hasten to rescue those whom you can. Seek by all means to save some. God the Holy Ghost awakens men; but he loves to use their fellowmen as his instruments.

Awake! awake! Sleeping world, awake! We tell of great realities. It is no dream that soothes our conscience and fills our heart. No, it is that greatest of all facts, that most solid of all truths, *'God so loved the world, that he gave his only begotten Son, that whosoever believeth in him should not perish'*,—no, not perish,—*'but have everlasting life'* (*John* 3:16). God, the eternal Son, came down into our world, in our nature; lived, suffered, and died, 'the Just for the unjust, to bring us to God'; and on the resurrection morning the Father sealed his work as all complete. Whoever receives this Saviour enters the family of God at once (*John* 1:12). Thousands upon thousands have in their own experience proved the reality and greatness of this salvation. They tell you that it is no dream that Christ the Saviour meets the cravings of the heart and conscience. It is no dream that Christ is 'altogether lovely'. It is no dream (they all accord in testifying) that 'he who cometh to him shall never hunger, and he that believeth on him shall never thirst' (*John* 6:35).

Lose no time, for the Lord is coming quickly to take vengeance on all who obey not the gospel (*2 Thess.* 1:8). Come and prove for yourself all we say. You shall have 'joy and peace in believing' (*Rom.* 15:13), and never more be in danger of the 'desolation' and appalling surprise of those who live upon their dreams. Come and try the Fountain open for sin. Come and reason with him who shows you how scarlet sins become white as snow (*Isa.* 1:18). Come and hear that most substantial and most satisfying of all truths, 'Jesus Christ came into the world to save sinners' (*1 Tim.* 1:15). 'By him, whosoever believeth is justified from all things' (*Acts* 13:39.) *Christ believed in* is peace to the soul, and true peace is no dream.

2

THE CUP OF WRATH

For in the hand of the Lord there is a cup, and the wine is red;
it is full of mixture; and he poureth out of the same:
but the dregs thereof, all the wicked of the earth
shall wring them out, and drink them.

Psalm 75:8

It will greatly help to the right apprehension of this solemn subject to notice that Christ is the speaker of these awful truths. They cannot, then, have been spoken harshly; they must have been uttered in all tenderness. As head of his church, Christ says (verse 1), 'Unto thee, O God, do we give thanks'; and then (verse 2), looking on a world lying in wickedness, he anticipates a different state of things ere long: 'I purpose when I shall receive the congregation that I shall judge uprightly.' This shall be in the day when he returns to judge the earth. It is he, meanwhile, who upholds all by the word of his power; he keeps the world from falling into ruin; he it is that sustains that blue firmament, as well as earth's foundations, 'I bear up the pillars thereof'—and were I to withhold my hand, all would tumble into ruin. Oh that an unthinking world would consider! Oh that fools would learn wisdom, and the proud fall down before their Lord. For the Judge shall surely come, with the cup of red wine in his hand—a cup of wrath, of which every rebellious one must drink to the dregs. The horns of the wicked

7

shall soon be laid low, and the righteous alone exalted (verse 10).

It is of this cup that we this day wish to speak to you. It gives an alarming, awakening view of our God and Saviour. It is not 'God in Christ reconciling the world to himself', but God the Judge, Christ the Judge. It is not the King with the golden sceptre, inviting all to draw near; it is the King risen up in wrath, in the evening of the day of grace, to 'judge all the wicked of the earth'.

Oh there is a hell, an endless hell, awaiting the ungodly! The Judge warns us of it in order that none of us may be cast into that tremendous woe. Say not in your hearts, 'God is too loving and merciful ever to condemn a soul to such woe.' If you continue in sin you shall know too late that the Judge does condemn; not because he is not infinitely loving, but because your sin compels him so to do. Listen to what is written, and you will see that as sure as ever an unworthy communicant drank the wine out of the cup, so surely, if unpardoned, he shall drink of this wine of God's indignation.

1. *The Cup of Wrath.* The general idea of the verse is, that there is wrath against sin to be manifested by God, terrible beyond measure. As it is written in Ezekiel 18:4, 'The soul that sinneth, it shall die'; and Psalm 7:11-13: 'God is angry with the wicked every day. If he turn not, he will whet his sword; he hath bent his bow, and made it ready. He hath prepared for him the instruments of death.' In Psalm 11:6-7: 'Upon the wicked he shall rain snares, fire and brimstone, and an horrible tempest: this is the portion of their cup. For the righteous Lord loveth righteousness.' In Psalm 21:9: 'Thou shalt make them as a fiery oven in the time of thine anger.' In Job 36:18: 'Because there is wrath, beware lest he take thee away with his stroke; then a great ransom cannot deliver thee.' In Romans 2:5 we read, 'Thou treasurest up unto thyself wrath against the day of wrath and revelation of the righteous judgment of God'; and in

Revelation 14:9-10: 'If any man worship the beast, the same shall drink of the wine of the wrath of God, which is poured out without mixture into the cup of his indignation; and he shall be tormented with fire and brimstone in the presence of his holy angels, and in the presence of the Lamb.' Can words be found more emphatic to express God's indignation at man's sin?

'A cup' is spoken of. A measured out portion (*Psa.* 11:5, and *Psa.* 16:5: 'The Lord is the portion of my cup.') It is frequently used to express 'a full amount;' as when the fulfilment of curse is called the 'cup of trembling' in Isaiah 51:22; and in Ezekiel 23:31-33, wrath upon Samaria is 'the cup of Samaria'. God's wrath shall be given forth in a measured portion, deliberately and fairly considered. There shall be nothing of caprice, nothing arbitrary, in God's judgment on sin; all shall be fairly adjusted. Here are the sins; there is the cup, of a size proportioned to the sin, and full. God's perfections direct and dictate the filling of it.

It is a *'cup of red wine'*. He elsewhere calls it 'The wine of my fury'; and in Revelation 16:19, it is 'wine of the fierceness of his wrath'. In the East, red wine was usually the strongest; but besides, the fiery nature of the contents is indicated by the colour. This 'red wine' is pressed out of the grapes by the divine attributes. It must be the concentrated essence of wrath; no weak potion, but one like that in Jeremiah 25:16, where they 'drink, and are moved, and are mad'; or that in Ezekiel 22:32-33: 'A cup deep and large; it containeth much; a cup of astonishment and desolation, filled with drunkenness and sorrow.'

It is *'full of mixture'*.—This signifies that the wine's natural quality has been strengthened; its force has been intensified by various ingredients cast into it. Such is the sense of 'mingled wine' in Isaiah 5:22, and in Proverbs 9:5, 'Come, drink of the wine which I have mingled.' We must distinguish this from the expression *'without mixture'*, in Revelation 14:10, where the speaker means to say, that there is no infusion of water to weaken the strength of the wine. Here there is everything that may enhance the bitterness of the cup; and let us ask, What may be these various ingredients? From every side of the lost sinner's nature forms of misery shall arise. The body, as well as soul, shall be steeped in never-ending anguish, amid the unceasing wretchedness of eternal exile and lonely imprisonment. Further, each attribute of Godhead casts something into the cup. *Righteousness* is there; so that the rich man in hell (*Luke* 16) dare not hint that his torment is too great. *Mercy and love* stand by and cast on it their ray, testifying that the sinner was dealt with in long-suffering, and salvation placed within his reach. O the aggravation which this thought will lend to misery. *Omnipotence* contributes to it; the lost man in the hands of the Almighty is utterly help-less, weak as a worm. *Eternity* is an ingredient, telling that this wrath endures as long as God lives. And *truth* is there, declaring that all this is what God spoke, and so cannot be altered without overturning his throne. Yet more: while shame and contempt, and the consciousness of being disowned by every holy being, fiercely sting the soul, there are ingredients cast in by the sinner himself. His *conscience* asserts and attests that this woe is all deserved, and the man loathes himself. *Memory* recalls past opportunities and times of hope despised. Sin goes on increasing, and passions rage; cravings gnaw the unsatisfied soul with eternal hunger. It may be that every particular sin will contribute to the mixture—a woe for broken Sabbaths; a woe for lusts gratified; a woe for every scoff, and every blasphemy and oath; a woe for every act of drunkenness, and every falsehood and dishonesty; a woe for every rejected invi-tation, and every threatening disregarded. Who can tell what more may be meant by the words: *'full of mixture'*?

It has *'dregs'* in it. The dregs lie at the bottom, out of sight, but are the bitterest. Do these mean hidden woes not yet conceived of by any? Such as may be hinted at in the words, 'Better he had never been born'? Such as Christ's woes seem to speak of? These shall be the reverse of the saved man's joys, 'which never have entered the heart' to imagine. Backsliders seem sometimes to have begun to taste these dregs. Apostates, like Spira, have shown a little of what they may be. But oh, the reality in the ages to come! For it shall be the wrath of him whose breath makes the mountains smoke, and rocks earth to its centre. O the staggering madness of despair!

'*He poureth out of the same.*' '*The wicked shall wring them out and drink them.*' They are not meant to be merely shown; this is not a cup whose contents shall only be exhibited and then withdrawn. No, the wicked must '*drink them*', and cannot refuse. When Socrates, the Athenian sage, was adjudged to drink the cup of poison, he was able to protest his innocence, and thus to abate the bitterness of the draught, though he took it as awarded by the laws of his country. Here, however, there shall be nothing like protest, nothing of any such alleviation of the awful draught which the sinner *must* drink. 'God poureth out', and the guilty soul '*shall wring out and drink*' the very dregs. Job 27:22, says, 'They would fain flee out of his hand', but cannot, for it is written, 'God shall cast upon him and not spare.' In Jeremiah 25:15-16, we have the Lord most peremptorily commanding, 'Take the wine-cup of this fury at my hand, and cause all the nations, to whom I send thee, to drink it. And they shall drink, and be moved and be mad.' And further, he insists, verse 28, 'If they refuse to take the cup at thine hand to drink, then shalt thou say unto them, Thus saith the Lord of hosts, Ye shall certainly drink.' 'They shall drink of the wrath of the Almighty' (*Job* 21:20). And what mean those words already quoted in Revelation 14:9-10? It shall not, on God's part, be a mere silent feeling of indignation at sin; there must be infliction of curse. There is no thunder while the electricity sleeps in the cloud. The seven seals showed no deliverance for earth while unbroken; the seven trumpets summoned no avengers, till sounded; the seven vials brought down no judgment, while only held in the angels' hands. Ah yes, the penalty must be exacted, and it will require eternity to exact it all!

O fellow-sinner, we have tried to say somewhat of this doom; but what are words of man? You have seen a porous vessel, in which was fine flavoured liquor? Outside you tasted the moisture, and it gave a slight idea of what was within; but slight indeed. So our words today. And remember, each new sin of yours will throw in more mixture. It is the merciful One himself who speaks in Ezekiel 22:13-14: 'Behold, I have smitten mine hand at thy dishonest gain which thou hast made, and at thy blood which hath been in the midst of thee. Can thine heart endure, or can thine hands be strong, in the days that I shall deal with thee? *I the Lord have spoken it and will do it.'* It is dreadful to read and hear this proclamation of wrath; but it is all given in order to compel us to flee from it. As one of our poets (Montgomery) sings:

> Mercy hath writ the lines of judgment there;
> None who from earth can read them need despair.

2. *The story of One who drank this cup to the dregs.* We would not leave you merely contemplating the terrors of that wrath. We go on, in connection with it, to speak of One whose history has a strange bearing on our case.

There has been only One who has ever 'drunk this cup *to its dregs.'* Cain has been drinking it for 5,000 years, and finds his punishment greater than he can bear, but has not come to the dregs. Judas has been drinking it for nearly 2,000, often crying out with a groan that shakes hell, 'Oh that I had never been born! Oh that I had never seen or heard of the Lord Jesus Christ!' But he has not reached the dregs. The fallen angels have not come near the dregs: for they have not arrived at the judgment of the Great Day. The only One who has taken, tasted, drunk, and wrung out the bitterest of the bitter dregs, has been *the Judge himself,* the Lord Jesus!

You know how often, when on earth, he spoke of it. 'Are ye able to drink of the cup that I shall drink of?' (*Matt.* 20:22.) 'The cup which my Father hath given me, shall I not drink it?' (*John* 18:11). In Psalm 88:15, 'I am afflicted and ready to die from my youth up: I suffer thy terrors: I am distracted.' The universe saw him with it at his lips. It was our cup of trembling; the cup in which the wrath due to the 'multitude which no man can number' was mingled. What wrath, what woe! A few drops made him cry, 'Now is my soul troubled!' In the garden, the sight of it wrung out the strange, mysterious words, 'Sorrowful unto death!' Though God-man, he staggered at what he saw, and went on trembling. Next day, on Calvary, he drank it all. I suppose the three hours darkness may have been the time when he 'was wringing out the dregs'; for then arose from his broken heart the wail that so appealed to the heart of the Father, 'My God, my God, why hast thou forsaken me?' As he ended the last drop, and cried out, 'It is finished', we may believe angels felt an inconceivable relief—and even the Father himself! So tremendous was the wrath and curse!—the wrath and curse due to our sin.

In all this, there was nothing too much. Love would protest against one drop too much; and never do you find our God exceeding. Did he not hasten to stay Abraham's hand when enough had been done on Moriah? and at that same spot again, in David's day, when Justice had sufficiently declared the sharpness of its two-edged sword, did he not again hasten to deliver, crying, 'It is enough'? How much more then when it was his beloved Son? He sought from Him all that was needed by justice; but would exact not one drop beyond what justice craved. And so we find in this transaction what may well be good news to us. For Jesus drank that cup as the substitute for the great 'multitude', his innumerable people, given him of the Father; and thereby freed them from ever tasting even one drop of that fierce wrath, that 'cup of red wine, full of mixture', with its dregs, its unknown terrors. Now, this One, this only One, who so drank the whole, presents to the sinners of our world the *emptied Cup*—his own Cup emptied. He sends it round the world, calling on mankind-sinners to take it and offer it to the Father as satisfaction for their sins. Come, O fellow-sinner, grasp it and hold it up to God! Plead it, and thou art acquitted.

Yes, if you are anxious at all to be saved and blessed, take up this emptied cup. However cold thy heart, however dull thy feelings, however slight thy sorrow for sin, take this emptied cup. Your appeal to this emptied cup arrests judgment at once. Do not think you need to endure some anguish of soul, some great sorrow—to take some sips of the red wine, far less to taste its dregs, ere you can be accepted. What thoughtless presumption! Imitating Christ in his atoning work! If Uzziah, the king, presenting incense when he ought to have let the priest do it for him, was smitten for his presumption, take care lest you be thrust away, if you presume to bring the fancied incense of your sorrow and bitter tears. It is the emptied cup that is offered us, not the cup wet with our tears, or its purity dimmed by the breath of our prayers. Feelings of ours, graces of ours, can do nothing but cast a veil over the perfect merits of Christ.

Man of God who hast used this cup, keep pleading it always. Ever make it the ground of thine assurance of acceptance. Examine it often and well—see how God was glorified here, and how plentifully it illustrates and honours the claims of God's righteousness. Full payment of every claim advanced by Justice is here; and so you, in using it, give good measure, pressed down and running over. What then remains but that you render thanks and take this salvation, often singing,

> Once it was mine, that cup of wrath,
> And Jesus drank it dry!

What should ever hinder thy triumphant joy? Be full of gratitude; and let this gratitude appear in thy letting others know what it has done for you, and may do for them.

For again we say to you, fellow-sinner, if you accept it not, soon you shall have no opportunity of choice. May I never see one of my people drinking this awful cup! May I never see it put into their hands! The groaning of a soul, dying in sin, is at times heard on this side of the veil, and it is the saddest and most haunting of all solemn and awful scenes; but what is that to the actual drinking of the cup, and wringing out the very dregs, that God 'poureth out of the same'. Never may Satan have it in his power to upbraid you with having once had the offer of salvation, an offer never made to him! It seems to me that; every Sabbath, specially, the Lord takes gospel-hearers aside into a quiet secluded nook, and there sets down before them the 'cup of red wine, full of mixture', and then the emptied cup of Jesus, earnestly, most earnestly, most sincerely, most compassionately, pressing them to decide and be blessed. Men and brethren, never rest till the Holy Ghost has in your eye so glorified Christ who drank the cup, that you see in him your salvation and God's glory secured beyond controversy, beyond even Satan's power to question or assail.

3

COMING TO CHRIST

The natural man is exceedingly perverse, and Satan knows how to wield this perversity of the heart. We, in our day, are ready to excuse ourselves for our slowness to believe in the Lord Jesus by saying, 'How much easier it would have been, had we seen him in the flesh, and been with him when he wrought his gracious works, and when he spoke his gracious words that were such as never man spake!' Now, in reality, they who then lived had by far the greater difficulties in the way of their faith. One whom no man honoured claims this service,—'Follow me.' One whom man despiseth says, 'I and the Father are one.' That rejected one, the by-word among the people, the song of the drunkard, stands in the temple and cries, 'If any man thirst, let him come *unto me* and drink!' and promises, 'He that believeth *in me,* out of him shall flow rivers of living water!'

In those days, the difficulty felt by his hearers, and by his very disciples, was to believe without a doubt that *this was the right person;* this Jesus the real Immanuel, the Saviour of the world. To these men there seems never to have occurred the thought that there was difficulty *in the act of coming,* or in knowing *what coming to him meant;* the difficulty they felt was the being sure that Jesus was the Christ. Only let that point be settled, and their souls are at rest.

Such was the state of things then. But now it is altered. Satan has shifted his ground, and tries to puzzle us with the questions, *'How are we to come?'* and *'What is meant by coming to Christ?'* We are in the habit of admitting that Christ's claims are beyond dispute; that he is God-man, and sent by the Father to be the propitiation for our sins. The reproach heaped on him when first he came is so far rolled away, that all professing disciples agree in never doubting for a moment (as they suppose) that Christ, and no other, is the Saviour to whom they are to come. But then the natural heart finds out a new hindrance in the way of at once resting satisfied in him. 'What do you mean by *coming?*' is a question often asked and dwelt upon; and many a soul says, 'If I only knew *how to come aright,* I would rejoice!'

Let us, then, ask what is the true state of the case; whether or not there be any barrier put in our way by this expression, 'Come.' Is it a mysterious act of the mind? Is it some very delicate feeling? Is it a great experience, or a high attainment, that must precede the enjoyment of Christ as ours?

In reply to such questions, I remark that nothing but a self-righteous tendency in the heart would ever have led us to mistake a matter which in itself is very simple. We repeat it—it is the self-righteousness of the natural man that leads him to think that there is anything perplexing in words which Christ thought so simple that he never once has given an explanation of them. For it is a fact, that just as our Master knew there was no need of explaining to anyone what he meant when he said, *'Hearken!'* so did he consider *'Come!'* to be a term that needed no explanation. Anyone that has an ear knows the former: why should anyone who has a soul that can think and feel not know the latter? It is self-righteousness that entangles us here; it is a want of sufficient appreciation of Christ. The hesitation arises from our sight of what Christ is being still very dim; not attractive enough to fill our heart and conscience.

For, in truth, this *'Coming to Christ'* is simply the soul's state when occupied with thoughts about Christ, so occupied therewith as to have left behind it all other things. The soul in such a state of engrossment, is said to have *come to him*. It has no other whom it cares for, no other that fills up its desires, no other that meets its case; and so it has left all others for this One, and in doing so is said to have '*come to him*'. His person and work have met the cravings of both conscience and heart.

If you are at all troubled with this 'Come', I do not hesitate to say that your eye is averted from its proper object. When Jesus says, '*Come unto me*' (*Matt.* 11:28), he never meant you to stop short at the first word; he meant you to put all the stress upon '*me*'. Indeed, he has used a form of expression that is purposely fitted to produce this result; for he has used a word for 'Come' which [in the Greek original] is neither more nor less than '*This way*', or '*Hither*',—not a verb, but an adverb. He cries, 'All ye that are heavy laden, leave off trying other means and try *me! This way* to me! *Hither* to me!' It is thus that he speaks, putting the whole stress upon '*me*'. 'All ye that labour', says the gracious Master, 'look *this way!* look *hither!* to *me*—to *Me*—to none other but to *me!*'

It is the same word used, John 21:12, 'Come and dine', where surely he meant not to say more or less than, 'Leave off now your other engagements, and let us dine.' It is the woman's word at Sychar, 'Come, see a man that told me all' (*John* 4:29). It is the Master's word in the parable (*Matt.* 22:4), 'Come to the marriage;' that is 'Let us off to the marriage! All is ready; away to this feast!' It is the angel's word at the tomb (*Matt.* 28:6), 'Come, see the place where the Lord lay'; that is, 'Here is the spot, see for yourselves; this way, down here!' So that the emphasis all lies in the object presented to us; never in the act of our minds. But we, self-righteous as we are, would fain delay and linger, excusing ourselves by saying, 'I do not know how to perform the act aright.' The real truth, however, is that we are not quite satisfied, or perhaps not *very fully occupied*, with the object. We would not thus tarry on our own feelings, and acts, and states of mind, were we very fully engrossed with the Christ who is set before us, and who stands in the abundance of his grace beckoning us to advance and enjoy infinite love; This way, O sinner! this way! To *me*, and to no other!'

Yes, this is all. He beckons you to himself! Why turn in your eye on yourself? why gaze on your wounds? why gaze on your temptations? why look at waves and listen to winds? The Master cries, 'To *me*, to *me*.' He says, O soul, up! forsake *your* schemes, *your* thoughts, *your* ways, and away at once to *me!* O precious soul! do not be detained by inquiries into the acts of your mind, but at once think of *me; me*, whom the Father sent to save sinners, even the chief; *me*, who came to seek and save the lost; *me*, whom the Spirit delighteth to glorify; *me*, who have satisfied the law, who my own self bare your sins in my own body on the tree; *me*, who have done all that a sinner needs for righteousness; *me*, who am come to give you myself, with all I have done and suffered, to be your ransom. Take *me* for your conscience; take *me* for your heart.

The case might be stated thus. When I, a sinner, am brought to be willing that Christ should come to me and give me all I need, this is my soul's coming to Christ. My coming to Christ is, in other words, my soul *satisfied with his coming to me!* When my soul is letting alone and forsaking other things, because *taken up with Christ's coming out of the Father's bosom* to save sinners; this is my soul's coming to Christ! My conscience was asking, 'Wherewithal shall I come before God?' Shall it be by bringing rivers of oil? Shall it be by offering my soul's sorrow and bitterest grief, as well as my body's penance? I find that it is not thus; nor yet by my prayers, nor by the help of any priest, nor by the aid of any creature's merit, nor by anything that is not to be found in Christ. *What is in Christ* is all that my soul needs. Perplexed soul, the Holy Spirit brings all such difficulties as yours to an end by fixing the attention and staying the mind upon this glorious truth, viz., That Christ, 'his own self' (*1 Pet.* 2:24), is the only atonement for sin, the only propitiation. Do think of Christ, his person, his heart of love, his words of grace, and all this in connection with his finished work, his sacrifice accepted; and while thus engaged, 'ere ever you are aware, your soul shall be as the chariots of Amminadib' (*Song of Sol.* 6:12).

Most blessed word, 'Come!'; but let it not be misunderstood. It is not itself the Leader, but only the waving of his banner, and the streaming of its folds to the four winds of heaven, as if saying, 'Gather to Shiloh, all ends of the earth.' Blessed word, 'Come!'; only remember, it is not itself Christ, but only his kind voice drawing off my attention from other objects. It is not the sacrifice, but it is the silver trumpet summoning me to the sacrifice. Blessed word, 'Come', for, instead of the tremendous, 'Depart!' of the judgment-day, spoken to rejecting and rejected sinners, it sends forth the proclamation of the gate still open, the heart of God open, for me a sinner.

But perhaps you object—'Surely I have something to do, for does he not go on to say, *'Take my yoke upon you,* and learn of me, and ye shall find rest to your souls'? (*Matt.* 11:29). Yes, he does, but he does not say that this taking on of his yoke is the same as *coming to him.* Far otherwise; it is what follows upon your coming to him; it is the service you engage in *after having come* to him. You come to him at once, and find rest at once; and on the spot he makes your soul as white as snow: and then, the next step is your drawing his plough, *'taking on his yoke'.* In thus serving and 'learning of him', you get *another rest,* viz. rest from former corruptions, passions, unholy impulses, tormenting desires. This *second* rest is the rest of Sanctification, and is not to be confounded with the first rest, which is that of Justification.

At once, then, fellow-sinner, hasten to him. All you need is here. Here is full salvation; for he says, 'All things are delivered unto me of my Father.' Here is free salvation; for the Father reveals it to whom he will, and nothing whatsoever in the sinner can be a barrier to him. It is a salvation all plain; for 'he reveals it unto babes.' It is a salvation all for sinners; for the persons invited are *'heavy-laden ones'*, persons who have a load of sin, whether they feel it little or much or not at all; and *'labouring'*, that is, trying in vain to save themselves, trying in vain to swim to shore.

Surely, then, I and Christ must meet. Why should we not? He beckons me off self and all else, and says, 'To *me*, to *me* alone!' This day, then, let it be so! Father, I see thee pointing me away from ordinances, from the Bible, from my faith, as well as from my unbelief, to *Christ alone,* that I and he may meet! the sinner and the Saviour! no one between! Jesus, Master, in *thee,* in *Thee,* is peace! Holy Spirit, thou hast bathed my weary soul! And here I rest, until the day arrive when I shall hear him say, 'Come, ye blessed of my Father, inherit the kingdom prepared for you before the foundation of the world.' I get rest the moment I come to him. I get rest again when I become somewhat like him, and the troubled sea of my passions sinks into a calm. I shall get a third rest when I die in the Lord (*Rev.* 14:13); and soon I shall enter on the final rest that remains for the people of God, when he to whom I now come shall come from heaven to glorify all who here came to him (*2 Thess.* 1:7).

4

LOVE THE LORD JESUS

Beloved Christian Friends,—It is not possible to take up this subject of 'Love to the Lord Jesus', without speaking at the same time of his love to us. If we want to warm a man benumbed with cold, we must bring him to the fire; and if we want to keep him warm, we must keep him at the fire. So I see no escape, with this programme before me, but to speak first about *his love to us*.

Let me begin by removing what might seem to be an imputation upon God's love to us, and which would interfere with our love to him. We read, 'I love them that love me' (*Prov.* 8:17): and then we read again this other word, 'We love him because he first loved us' (*1 John* 4:19). The two passages do not seem consistent with each other. But Solomon was too wise in the things of God, and the Holy Ghost who inspired his words knew too well the mind of God, to make any mistake. And John, who lay in his Master's bosom, knew it all well, and it is he who says, 'He first loved us.' The analogy of a parent's love explains the whole. The parent loves the child long before the child understands what love is; but as the child grows up, its love, drawn out by the parent's love for it, and shown in daily acts of filial obedience, draws forth new and special manifestations of love for the delighted parent. Even so, it is quite true, 'He first loved us'; and it is also quite true that, when we keep his commandments, his love is manifested to us more and more in peculiar tenderness (*John* 14:21).

There is a passage in John's Epistle that is sometimes applied to the children of God to their hurt. It is this, 'Perfect love casteth out fear' (*1 John* 4:18). Some give that away to the disciple: now I claim it for my Lord. In the original there is an article before the word 'perfect', so that it reads, '*The* perfect love casteth out fear.' And where was perfect love manifested but on Calvary? Beloved friends, faith learns that love, faith apprehends that love; and if you would have victory over fear, it is by seeing this perfect love, and its manifestation on the Cross. There it shines in noon-day splendour. It is not your love that is meant; that, however real, will not be perfect here. And if you say, 'You forget John has already said, 'Herein is our love made perfect' (*1 John* 4:17), I claim this also for the Lord. Look at the margin. It is, 'Herein is *the* love *with us* made perfect.' It is the love of God come down from heaven to us; it is Immanuel-love. The apostle says, 'Herein the love which came down from heaven into our hearts is made perfect.' And this expression, 'is made perfect', has the same meaning as when the Lord Jesus used it concerning himself in Luke 13:32, 'The third day I shall be perfected'; and as in Hebrews 2:10, 'The Captain of our salvation made perfect through suffering.' *Fully installed into effect* is the meaning in these places. And so also here the meaning is—the love of God reaches its goal, or is installed into its full office, when it enables the believer to have boldness in the day of judgment. As long as you have fear in your heart, you have not fully apprehended that perfect love of God. Take in that perfect love of God manifested in Christ, and you will have boldness in the day of judgment—in the day of his Coming which is drawing near. Yes, you will have boldness in that day, when the wicked shall cry to the rocks and mountains to hide them from the face of the Lamb. The saints, ascending from the tomb, shall say, 'Lo, this is our God; we have waited for him.' There is nothing but boldness for us in that day, not because of our love to him, but because of his love to us.

Having thus cleared our way, let me remind you of some things said about this love in the Old Testament. You remember that passage in the Song (chap. 8:6), 'Love is strong as death; jealousy is cruel as the grave, &c.' Who says this? It is the Bride, as she leans on the Bridegroom. She says, 'I know of a love stronger than death.' It is his love that is stronger than death. Death is stronger than all things but God. It overcomes all on earth; but Christ's love is stronger still. There is no barrier in its way which it will not break down. Guilt and sin he put out of the way by the Cross; the corruption of our heart he overcomes by his Holy Spirit, and nothing can separate us from that love of his. Many years ago, Mr Andrew Gray (whose memory is fragrant in this city) and Dr Malan were talking together about the grace of God. Dr Malan suddenly said, 'Brother, you would not go to heaven if you could help it; but, brother, you must and shall go.' Mr Gray was somewhat startled; but Dr Malan, in his own way, was giving emphatic expression to the truth, that it is just the infinite strength of this Love—Love that will never unloose its grasp which keeps a believer, in spite of earth and hell and his own corruption.

Then, further, it is 'jealous love'; for that is the meaning of 'jealousy cruel as the grave.' It will not be interfered with; it must have the whole heart. He is determined you shall be all his and his alone. He seeks the whole heart. And it looks often cruel, that jealous love of his. He will send you trials, he will sweep away idols; sore afflictions and bereavements come, and he seems deaf as the grave to your tears and mourning cries. But it is all love. It is his jealous love—the heart-love of God which would not let you hurt yourself by putting another object in his place.

Then, it has 'coals of fire'. There is intense heat in it, a fervour worthy of God. And so (as it stands in the Hebrew) it is said to be 'Like coals of fire, *Jehovah's flame*', most vehement. It is the flame of Jehovah, as if no other comparison could be found for it. It is

Jehovah's affection, Jehovah's loving heart. Do you not feel ashamed of the coldness of your hearts when you think of his?

Then, its manifestation is only beginning now. It is in the ages to come he is to show the exceeding riches of his grace in his kindness toward us (*Eph.* 2:7). These ages begin when the Lord shall return; we are only in the dawn yet; and if the dawn be so wondrous, what will the noon of glory be? Does it not set your heart a tingling to think of this Love? Many waters could not quench it, and many 'floods cannot drown it.' The objects of that love were sinners, against every one of whom could be established the charge of guilt most heinous, rebellion, enmity, ignorance, base ingratitude, folly, pollution; yet his love was not cooled, far less quenched. And when Satan offered him all earth's glory at once, if he would forego his errand of redeeming love, he did 'utterly despise' the offer.

Now, then, what is your love to him in return? Is it *'strong'* as death? Could you face death for him? I do not mean merely could you die once for him—but is your love strong as death every day? Is it such as can face the world and your own corruption every day, and not be overcome? A martyr's death is not the worst death after all. By far the sorest is the daily victory over the flesh and the world. In Germany, some time ago, I saw a terrible instrument of torture called 'The Maiden', which opened to take in its victims, and with rows of sharp-pointed spikes closed on them, piercing head and heart through and through. I don't doubt but that you could face that appalling death; for, beloved friends, it is not so difficult to face that death *once* as it is to live *every day* in the midst of cold-hearted professors, and keep a glowing heart to Christ all the time.

Then, is your love to Christ a *'jealous'* love? His is jealous towards you. Are you on the watch against the world getting into his place? And is it easily cooled? Many such questions we might ask, if time permitted.

But, for a moment longer, let me take you to a New Testament passage. Look at Ephesians 3:17: 'Rooted and grounded in love', the apostle says. The believer's roots are in it. Look at that! And when Paul prays that with all saints we 'may be able to comprehend what is the breadth, and length, and depth, and height'; it is as if he had said, If you wish to know what *height* is, try to scale the heights of this love. If you wish to know what *depth* is, try to fathom this love. If you would know what *length* and *breadth* mean, try to measure this love. You will only reach thus far, viz., you will perceive that it 'passes knowledge'.

In Paul's day, the mist that had for ages rested on this ocean had risen. And what had they discovered? God-man, the Christ of God, the mighty Sacrifice, laid on the altar! He bore the fire, and bore the curse, and bore the Father's expression of his hatred against sin. 'Herein indeed was love' (*1 John* 4:10). O man of God, look at this cross and see his love. Study that love which you are to study for ever, and press on to that day when you shall know it as you never can know it here. And stir up others to join with you, for this love is best studied 'with all saints', each one helping the other.

I close by asking you, beloved, do you cultivate the meditation of that love in your heart? If there be one here who wishes to quench unholy love, this love will do it; and if there be one who seeks to have more brotherly-love and love to all men, it is here his heart is set on fire. 'Whom having not seen we love'! and how then shall we love him when we see him and are with him for ever! Do you ever feel like Samuel Rutherford, when he says,

> O Thou the Father's eternally-sealed Love! O Flower and Bloom of heaven and earth's love, give me leave to stand beside Thy love, and look on and wonder. O Love, slain and crucified for me, give me leave to love Thee! at least, give me leave to wish to love Thee, if I can do no more.

5

THE HOLY SPIRIT

At the time when I first was enabled to say, 'Christ is mine', I recollect I had some mistaken ideas about the Holy Spirit. I had a secret feeling that I could not count so much upon his kindness as upon the Father's kindness, or the Son's. I thought he might be more easily grieved, or might go away for some little offence. I soon discovered, however, that this was a complete mistake. There is no love so mighty as the Spirit's love,—no love which will bear so much with us except the love of the Father and of the Son. I began to love him in another manner than before,—to love him much. Let me ask you, Do you positively love the Spirit?— Do you ever feel a glow of love to him who has done so much for you in your conversion?—who loves you and bears with you so much? You know it is he who has written the Bible,—every line of the Bible,—and therefore all about the love of God that you find there. Now, have you not often taken a letter which was sent you from a very kind friend, and shown it to one you love, your companion, saying, 'Did you ever read a letter like that? I can't tell you what I feel to the friend who wrote that letter.' And is it not thus you feel toward the Holy Ghost? I sometimes wonder if, when Christ has come, and we have been a little time with him in the kingdom,—I wonder if we shall not get the opportunity of personally and directly thanking the Holy Ghost. Sometimes I feel great love to the Spirit. I know I should, and I am sure all should, so feel always.

But, coming more directly to the subject before us tonight. Two disciples, you recollect, were on a memorable occasion on their way to the village of Emmaus, talking about him who they thought was to have been their Redeemer. As they were thus talking, Jesus himself drew near and walked with them, probably coming gently between them. Engrossed with the subject, they never turned to gaze at him. He, on his part, 'beginning at Moses and all the prophets, expounded unto them in all the Scriptures the things concerning himself',—and at length came into the house. Then, as he was breaking bread, he vanished from their sight. It was after he was gone, and only then, that they discovered and took notice of who had been with them. It seems to me we may find here a helpful illustration of the way in which the Holy Ghost acts and manifests himself when he is leading a sinner to Christ. When you, brother, were awakened, you were anxious to have clear views of the gospel. You had difficulties, and you spoke of them to some friend, who tried to clear away your misconceptions with little success. You and your friend were like Cleopas and his friend (*Luke* 24:18). But one came in between you both. The Holy Ghost came in between you both as you conversed together. He made the scales fall from your eyes, and at one point of the conversation, in a moment, you saw clearly the sinner's way to God. You did not, however, know, or at least you did not consider, that it was the Spirit who had touched your eyes, and opened them; and perhaps you now think the Holy Spirit must have been angry with you, because you did not take your thoughts off the Saviour and fix them on him. No: no more than Jesus was angry with the Emmaus disciples, because they did not know him. But do you remember that when you got Jesus to come in and sup with you, then you began to think of how all this change had come about? You now began to discover who it was that had been with you, and that he who had led you to Christ was still with you, still in the house, in the temple of your heart.

Jesus vanished out of the sight of the two disciples, leaving them for a time; but the Spirit does not leave those whom he has aided. Our comparison fails here; for when the Spirit has come into your heart he says, 'This is my rest. Here will I stay, for I do like it well.' No sooner is a soul sprinkled with the blood of Christ, to whom he has led the sinner, than the Spirit says, 'I will stay here for ever. I will never let this soul forget Christ.' Be sure of this,—the Spirit that led you to Christ is in you tonight; and now I want to show you some of the ways he is working in you.

1. One of the things he is doing is, he is *sealing* you. This you will find in Ephesians 1:13; 'In whom ye also trusted, after that ye heard the word of truth, the gospel of your salvation; in whom also, after that ye believed, *ye were sealed* with that Holy Spirit of promise'—the Holy Spirit promised to Christ by the Father, and promised by Christ to us. Let me dwell specially on one view of the *seal*. Wherever a seal is mentioned in Scripture, you find that it is something that everybody can see. Everybody could see the seal on the mouth of the cave, when Daniel was cast into the den of lions. I have no doubt the men who put Daniel in would look more than once during the night to make sure that the seal had not been broken. It would be a seal, perhaps with the king's likeness on it, or, at any rate, with his name; and this seal, which was wont to be stamped on a document, would, in the case of the den, be stamped upon softened clay. The king's face and the king's name being on it, no one would venture to break the seal, and everyone could see it. It was in a similar manner, when Christ was laid in the sepulchre, the Pharisees and elders put the seal of Rome on the stone, and no doubt visited the tomb more than once or twice, to see that it was there. And so with other 'sealings', such as that in Revelation 7:1-3, and similar cases.

We apply this fact about the seal to the passage before us (*Eph.* 1:13). The Lord puts a seal upon his own, that everybody may know them; and this is done (says the passage) *'after you believed'*. Something took place after you were converted, viz., you were *sealed*. This must mean something that marks you out to the observation of the world as God's people; it must mean something that the world can see. The Roman Governor, the Pharisees, any one, could look upon the seal on the Sepulchre; and so the world can see you to be sealed ones. The sealing in your case is the Spirit producing in you likeness to the Lord,—to the King and to the King's Son. If the likeness of Christ appear in you, shining out in your character, in your life, in your exhibiting the mind that was in Christ in you, and bearing in your person some resemblance to the Son of God,—that is the sealing. You have got the seal of God on you when you exhibit likeness to God's Son. The holier you become the seal is the more distinct and plain, the more evident to every passer-by, for then will men take notice of you that you have been with Jesus. A seal like that spoken of in Revelation 7:3, 'on the forehead', is yours. The sealing is something that cannot be hid. It is not even on the palm of your hand. It is in your forehead: all men see that you are not what you once were. The world takes notice that you are like what they have heard Jesus was. Whenever that takes place, the sealing is begun, and it remains all your lifetime, and becomes more and more plain. Every believer is thus 'sealed'.

2. But now we go on to another work of the Spirit in you. The passage says, he is *'the earnest of our inheritance'*. Here is a second view of the Holy Spirit in the same passage:—The Spirit the Seal, but the Spirit also *the Earnest*. Three times in the Epistles the Holy Spirit is called the earnest. You all know what an earnest is, the same that in Scotland we call 'arles'. It is different from the pledge—or the pawn; for the pawn or the pledge may be anything left in the room of another, and, when you bring the value of it, you get back the pledge. But it is not so with the earnest. In the 'earnest' you get nothing back, for it is a part, a small part, of what you are going to

get in great abundance afterwards. Is it not common, when anyone is hired as a servant, to give them arles—it may be a shilling, and they are to get ten pounds, that is, two hundred shillings, when the time for full wages comes—that shilling is arles, or earnest. Even so the Spirit is the earnest of our inheritance—he gives us the beginning of what we are to possess in full. And carefully notice this, viz. that just as the seal is outward, so the earnest is inward. The world cannot see the earnest; but you can, for you feel it. The world cannot know what passes within you; but you know, and this earnest is the beginning of your enjoyment of the glorious inheritance. When the Israelites were in the desert, and coming near the land of Canaan, twelve spies were sent into the land, who brought back great clusters of figs and pomegranates, and one bunch of grapes from Eshcol so large that it could be carried only by two men bearing it on a staff. Think for a moment of the spies laying these down—figs, pomegranates, and delicious-grapes—on the dry desert before all the people! 'That is a taste of what the land is', they would say. 'That is a sample, an earnest of the land.' Moses would say to Aaron, 'Taste that pomegranate.' And Aaron would hand some of the large grapes, deliciously juicy, to Miriam, and say, 'When we get to the land, we shall have whole orchards of pomegranates like this, and figs, and whole vineyards—mile upon mile, and acre upon acre—of such clusters of grapes!" Even so the Spirit comes into your heart, and gives you peace and joy as you look on Christ, and grace for grace out of his fullness; but yet all is only the earnest of what is to come. 'Still there's more to follow.' This is just a taste of what you will get in boundless abundance for ever and ever. The Spirit gives you this for your own enjoyment. It is all in yourselves. Your neighbour, your fellow-believer, does not share the same earnest of these things. Some believers get more of it, some less of it, but all get some. If what you have got is a taste of heaven, will you be content with that kind of heaven? Is that the holy, pure joy your soul longs for? Is this begun heaven so satisfying that you say, 'Only let me have more of this, and nothing of earth shall over tempt me away to any broken cistern?' The more of this earnest we have, the more we are weaned from the world. I am sure that when Moses and Aaron and the princes of Judah were refreshed by the taste of those delicious grapes, they would say one to another, 'Well, we won't care much for the desert now. We will weary for Canaan. What will the land be, if this is a sample of it?' Young believers, this is what the Spirit delights to give. This earnest he gives not only on special occasions—not only at the communion table—he gives it every day in the week. He gives it as you meditate on the Word. He gives it as you pray. He may sometimes do it when you are walking on the street. I remember in my first days of fellowship with Christ, being greatly interested by the experience of an aged Christian whom some of us often met as he walked along the North Bridge in Edinburgh. He sometimes moved along the crowded street, holding his hat a little above his head: and when asked the reason of this peculiar custom, he said, 'As I am walking along the streets, there are times when I get such glimpses of the Lord, and the communion is so sweet, that I cannot but take off my hat in reverence—His presence is so near!'

If, then, there are such earnests given, what will the kingdom be? There is the *seal* for others to look at: there is the *earnest* for yourselves to enjoy. 'Grieve not the Holy Spirit of Christ', for by him 'we are sealed till the day of redemption' (*Eph.* 4:30); and who is also 'the earnest' till the redemption-day has come (*Eph.* 1:14). Remember, he has not shown you as yet anything more than the mere beginnings. And let me add this other thought, before passing from this topic. Go back to the Spirit in the Old Testament symbols. At Christ's baptism (*Matt.* 3:16) the Spirit came down 'as a dove', and abode upon him. Why as the dove? You might say, because of its gentleness; even as Christ is the Lamb of God.

But the gentleness of the Lamb is only a small part of the truth in Christ's case, and so also the idea of gentleness is only a small part of the truth in the case of the dove. Go back to *Noah's dove* (*Gen.* 8:11), and what it brought to the ark—the olive leaf plucked off from some tree that was now above the water. The bringing of that leaf from the olive tree was meant to tell that the flood was over,—that a New Earth was appearing. Now, this is what the Spirit does as the earnest. He is the dove bringing us tidings of the deluge of wrath past, and of the New Earth ready to appear. He is always bringing us tidings of both wrath past and glory coming. The earnest he gives of peace and joy and love, and blessedness, are olive leaves plucked from the trees of the New Earth.

3. But let us speak of another view of the Spirit's working in us. It is this, The same Spirit is the *Intercessor* in your soul. He is the Sealer, the Earnest, and he is, at the same time, *the Intercessor* in your hearts (*Rom.* 8:26). 'Likewise the Spirit also helpeth our infirmities.' (Notice in passing here: Christ is touched with a feeling of our infirmities, and that is love; but the Spirit 'helpeth our infirmities'—surely that also is love. You see his kindness. He not merely feels for us, but he helps us.) *'For we know not what we should pray* for as we ought; but the Spirit himself *maketh intercession* for us with groanings that cannot be uttered.' There are times you know what to pray for, times when you see what things to ask; but in times of trouble, to which specially the text points, when we do not know what to say—whether to say, Take this thorn in my flesh away, or, Help me to bear it—the Spirit makes intercession for us with unutterable groanings. But note further, *'groaning desires'* is the full meaning; and these he raises in us on a thousand occasions, when we might have been content to be still, or would have sent forth our desires in another form. Only think of his kindness! He wants us to pray much, and for many things, for there is an answer to every such prayer; and so he says, 'I will come into your heart, I

will fill you with groanings that cannot be put into words; and he that searcheth the hearts will take them up and show them to the Father, and you shall get a large answer.' There is a line of a hymn, sometimes printed in a wrong way—

> Nor prayer is made *on earth alone*—
> The Holy Spirit pleads:
> And Jesus, on the eternal throne,
> For sinners intercedes.

It ought to be

> Nor prayer is made *by man alone*—

For that other line seems to say that the Spirit pleads in heaven, whereas he does not plead for us in heaven, but here on earth, by enabling us to pray for ourselves. When you pray, do you often say, 'Let the Spirit enable me to pray; let me pray in the Spirit'? Does the Spirit dictate your prayer? You will find it is often wonderfully helpful to look up to the Spirit to enable you to groan. Oh this love of the Spirit! How he helps!—the Spirit the Sealer, the Spirit the Earnest, the Spirit the Intercessor within us teaching us what to pray for, and how to pray; while Christ at the right hand takes up the prayer and sends the answer. Indeed, he is never done working in us; he is never for a moment letting us alone; he is always in some form taking the things of Christ and showing them to us.

4. Add to all this one other thought, What is '*the Communion of the Holy Ghost*'? (*2 Cor.* 13:14). Will you not henceforth love the Spirit more? Christ called him 'the other Comforter'—the Comforter who is every way like himself, who is with us from day to day, who abides with us for ever. Let us honour him; let us delight in him; let us cast the crown at his feet, the crown of salvation. Is not his loving-kindness infinite?

6

NEVER FORGIVEN

The Lake of Galilee was a favourite resort of the wealthy from various parts of the land. It was a region of forest and fruit trees, gardens and luxuriant orchards. Cool breezes from the lake and its hills refreshed the loungers on shore, and filled the sails of the pleasure boat as it glided among the innumerable fishes that dimpled the surface of the blue waters.

Among others who had come to this spot were 'Scribes from Jerusalem' (*Mark* 3:22), and Pharisees, all of them bitterly opposed to Christ. Hearing the people tell how he had cast out many devils at Capernaum (1:34; 3:11), they were irritated at his fame and influence, and when unable to deny the facts, suggested that these miracles were performed by the aid of Hell. *It is by Beelzebub*', lord of the hosts of hell,[1] *'that he casts out devils.'* When the report of their malicious insinuations reached the ear of Jesus, he seems to have resolved at once to confront them and seek to disarm them. *'He called them unto him'* (3:23), that is, he invited[2] them into the house. As appears from verses 31, 32, he got the use of the public room for this purpose, his mother and brethren retiring for a time. There, then, he sat in the midst of these Scribes and Pharisees, his disciples listening. There were many persons present, for verse 32 calls them 'a multitude', so that probably the room was full.

[1] If we take 'Beelzebul', the other reading of the MSS, the name signifies *Lord of Filth*', a name given to Satan in scorn and contempt.
[2] 'Called them unto him'—the same words that we find (*Matt.* 18:2) when he wished the little boy to come.

He explained to them why he had invited them to this some-what private interview; and then, after speaking of Satan's policy in keeping perfect unity among his hosts, a compact phalanx, and pointing out the absurdity of supposing that Satan would cast out Satan, he came to the main point, viz., what was involved in their attack upon him. 'Verily I say unto you' (verse 28), was his solemn manner of address; 'all sins shall be forgiven to the sons of men, and blasphemies wherewith they shall blaspheme'; or, as given in Matthew 12:31, 'All manner of sin and blasphemy.' He added, 'Whosoever speaketh a word against the Son of man, it shall be forgiven him'; as if to prevent them supposing there was anything personal in his words, proceeding from resentment at their unkind words. It is at present the lot of the Son of man to meet with the contradiction of sinners; his humiliation-state exposes him to mis-understanding; and while sin of this sort is still sin, and blasphemy, or insulting words, of this sort must still be blasphemy; yet there is forgiveness for such sin.

'But'—now take special notice—'He that shall blaspheme against the Holy Ghost hath never forgiveness, but is in danger of (is exposed to) eternal damnation (Mark 3:29). He is exposed at any moment to the doom of never-ending wrath; he is tottering on the brink of a tremendous precipice, over which if he falls nothing but everlast-ing woe is his portion. 'He hath never forgiveness'; he has no hold on pardon (οὐκ ἔχει ἄφεσιν), just as 1 John 5:12, says, 'He has not life', he has no hold of it; he shakes it off from him by his course of action.

In Matthew 12:32, the sentence runs, 'Whosoever speaketh against the Holy Ghost, it shall not be forgiven him'; and then, as equivalent to the 'eternal' doom mentioned by Mark, it is added, 'neither in this world, nor in that which is to come.' No pardon for such, the door is shut against them, never to be opened. It is shut even in this world: it shall remain shut to all eternity.

He gave this warning to these 'Scribes and Pharisees', *because* they said, 'He hath an unclean spirit' (*Mark* 3:30). And this warning of our Lord Satan has used in all ages to harass anxious souls and puzzle tender consciences. As if enraged at the Master for solemnly denouncing him and his ways, Satan has plied this saying against the peace and the hopes of very many who have not perceived the Lord's aim and meaning. It is altogether essential that we take it in connection with the circumstances in which it was spoken, in that room at Capernaum, in the course of that special interview with these 'Scribes from Jerusalem'.

In attempting to ascertain the nature of this unpardonable sin, this 'sin' or 'blasphemy against the Holy Ghost', we are on firm ground when we say,—

1. *It is not a sin that exhausts the virtue of Christ's blood.*

No sin is too great for that precious blood; it has power to cleanse from *all* sin (*1 John* 1:7). It is needless to enlarge on this truth, for all are agreed on this point: 'all manner of sins and blasphemies' can be at once washed away by it, whenever it is applied.

But the sin in our passage is never brought into contact with this blood. The person who commits the sin against the Holy Ghost is not one who shall be seen sitting mournfully at the Fountain open for sin, in vain applying its waters. It is not said here or anywhere that a person may go thither and return in despair because his sin was found to be too great; no, the passage speaks of a person who never goes thither at all. He never tests its power. It is not that he looked to the Brazen Serpent but in vain; no, but he would not deign to try that cure.

The man who commits this 'blasphemy against the Holy Ghost', is not one who tried the Saviour's blood, and has found no place for his guilty soul at the cross. On the contrary, he is one who is alienated from Christ; who hates Christ in his heart; who tries to find out reasons why he should not own him or accept him as his Saviour; who puts aside all the testimony borne to him. It is not that he has searched the Promised Land, and is compelled to declare it all a fable and delusion; no, but he is one who refuses to believe that there is any such Land, and therefore never sets out to seek it. It is not that he ran to the city of refuge and found its gates closed; but that he refused to run thither at all. The blood of the Lamb never loses its power; it succeeds in cleansing every sin brought to it. 'Though your sins be as scarlet, they shall be as white as snow; though they be red like crimson, they shall be as wool' (*Isa.* 1:18). What else could be true when the blood is the blood of 'Jesus Christ his Son'? As the snowflake disappears for ever at the touch of the furnace-flame, so does each sin when brought to the blood of Christ. But,

2. *It is a sin that exhausts the long-suffering of God.*

It puts an end to God's waiting and striving with the man. And so it occurs only in cases *where the Holy Spirit has been long at work* striving with the soul. To keep this view in mind is of the utmost importance.

It is in no case an isolated, solitary sin; a single act, however vile and wicked. A single act was never known to exhaust God's patience and long-suffering. It cannot, then, be an accidental word wrung from a soul in distress, or escaping the lips in an hour of fierce temptation. John Bunyan was wrong here, as he afterwards discovered; for on one occasion he gave way to Satan's persistent temptation, and in a weary, dark, hopeless mood of mind, said, 'Yes', when urged again and again to sell Christ. He thought on this account that all was over; that he had committed the unpardonable sin; that there was for him no forgiveness for ever. But the event proved his mistake; God's patient waiting on him was not exhausted, nor did the Spirit leave him.

Let us give in full the instance referred to in which Bunyan mistook his own case. He relates it thus:

One morning, as I lay in my bed, I was most fiercely assaulted with this temptation, viz., to sell and part with Christ—the wicked suggestion still running in my mind, 'Sell him! sell him! sell him!' as fast as a man could speak. Against which also, in my mind, as at other times, I answered, 'No, no, not for thousands, thousands',—at least twenty times together. But at last, after much striving, even until I was almost out of breath, I felt this thought pass through my heart, 'Let him go if he will!' and I thought also that I felt my heart freely consent thereto. Oh, the diligence of Satan! Oh, the desperateness of man's heart! Now was the battle won, and down fell I (as a bird that is shot from the top of a tree) into great guilt and fearful despair! Then, getting out of bed, I went moping into the field; but God knows with as heavy a heart as mortal man, I think, could bear. There, for the space of two hours I was like a man bereft of life; and as now past all recovery, and bound over to eternal punishment. And withal, that Scripture did seize upon my soul—'Profane person, as Esau, who for one morsel of meat sold his birthright! For ye know that afterward, when he would have inherited the blessing, he was rejected; for he found no place of repentance though he sought it carefully with tears' (*Heb.* 12:16, 17). Now was I as one bound; I felt myself shut up unto the judgment to come. Nothing now, for two years, would abide with me but an expectation of damnation; I say, nothing would abide with me but this, save some few moments of relief.

And thus, he went on, as if in fetters of brass. 'But one day', says he,

about ten or eleven o'clock of that day, as I was walking under a hedge, full of sorrow and guilt, bemoaning myself for this last hour, suddenly this sentence rushed in upon me, 'The blood of Christ remits all guilt.' At this I made a stand in my spirit. With that, this word took hold upon me, 'The blood of Jesus Christ his Son cleanseth us from all sin' (*1 John* 1:7).

Assuredly John Bunyan was forgiven; so that it is clear that vile and blasphemous thoughts and fancies, even if accompanied by the utterance of words that are equally vile and blasphemous, do not exhaust God's patience. Nor does every deliberate sin against clear light. The Lord can pity; the Holy Spirit can bear and forbear. Look at the whole nation worshipping the Golden Calf under the light of the Pillar-Cloud, and yet the Lord did not cast them away. Or listen to the horrid and malicious blasphemies of a most malignant foe in the case of Saul of Tarsus, who had sat under the heavens opened when Stephen was stoned at his feet, and who, even after that day, recklessly rushed on, causing others to utter blasphemies as vile as his own, all in spite of clear light. And yet he was forgiven.

The sin of our passage, then, is not an isolated act, but a sin occurring in *a course of sin*. This seems clear; and let us add, it occurs only in cases where resistance to the Holy Spirit is persistently offered. The Holy Spirit, in certain cases of this latter kind, ceases to strive, and altogether forsakes the soul. In the case before us, the case of these 'Scribes from Jerusalem' who were sitting with Christ in that room, and with whom he was so kindly remonstrating, this sin would be committed by them (he lets them know) if they went on in the present reckless course, scoffing and reviling. 'It is all from Satan!' He warns them that they would find themselves forsaken of the Spirit; left in the state described in Psalm 81:12, 'So I gave them up unto their own hearts' lust', and again, in Romans 1:28, 'As they did not like to retain God in their knowledge, he gave them over to a reprobate mind.'

We repeat it. In our passage, the Lord warns those with whom he is dealing that, inasmuch as he had told them that he cast out devils *'by the Spirit of God'*, and that therefore *'the kingdom of God was come nigh unto them'* (*Matt.* 12:28), they exposed themselves to the danger of being left in their sins, given over to eternal damnation, if they went a step further in their scoffing derision. They were virtually assailing the Holy Spirit who was striving with them, doing their utmost to get him to cease his striving; and so they would find themselves left in their sin, left in their guilt, left without the blood that pardons. Take warning, ye Scribes from Jerusalem, and ye Pharisees! the grieved Spirit may go away for ever, and ye will in that case never have a desire for pardon from the Saviour. If it be asked why he did not more directly say that such a man would 'grieve away the Spirit', the reason may have been that the full discovery of the Holy Spirit's work was not yet made; as we find stated in John 7:39. And perhaps the Lord had also some special reference to what was soon to be witnessed in Jerusalem. At present the Son of man in his low estate was reviled and rejected; but the Holy Spirit was to testify of him at Pentecost ere many months had passed, and who ever then should go on in his course of resistance must run the risk of being given up to a reprobate mind.

Isaiah 22:12-14, if not parallel, is, at least, analogous to this case: 'In that day did the Lord God of hosts call to weeping, and to mourning—and behold joy and gladness. And it was revealed in mine ear by the Lord of hosts, Surely this iniquity shall not be purged from you till ye die, saith the Lord God of hosts.' As if he had said: The grieved Spirit will forsake you, and so you shall be left in a state of alienation from God, which shall end in your never all your days being purged from this sin. And so Ezekiel 24:13, 'Because I have purged thee, and thou wast not purged, thou shalt not be *purged from thy filthiness any more.'* The Lord ceases to press them to accept the provided cleansing, and so they go on ever more in their filthiness. It is as if he had said, 'I have so often offered to purge thee, and thou hast so often refused, that now I shall let thee alone, and shall no more again bring pardon within thy reach; but shall cause my fury to rest upon thee.' It may be awfully perilous to let one other drop fall into the cup. A thousand times before this warning, you may have sinned, and yet all is not lost. But now beware—one more such sin, and who can tell but it may drive the Holy Spirit away for ever? You may have ascribed Christ's works to the devil again and again, and yet be forgiven; but if now, when warned, you go on persisting in this course, all is over! you are left by the Spirit to your own evil heart.[1]

3. *Some inferences fitted to relieve tender consciences.*

First. Some fear that they may fall into this sin altogether unwittingly and unconsciously, and they sometimes point to the case in 1 John 5:16,17. But *'the sin unto death'* in that passage, is not at all of the same sort with the unpardonable sin; for in it nothing is said of *'blasphemy against the Holy Ghost'*. No; it is a case like that in 1 Corinthians 11:30; where not the loss of the soul, but temporal chastisement, in the form of disease and death, overtook the sinning believer, for some special sins. It is not unlike what befell Uzzah in 2 Samuel 6:7, for a rash act that threatened to give wrong ideas of the God of Israel. The averting of this temporal chastisement was not to be prayed for; just as Moses was forbidden to ask the reversing of the judgment on his public sin: 'The Lord was wroth with me and would not hear me: and the Lord said unto me, Let it suffice thee; *speak no more unto me of this matter'* (*Deut.* 3:26). As Jeremiah also was, on a special occasion, expressly told, 'Pray not thou for this people, neither lift up cry nor prayer for them, neither make intercession to me: for I will not hear thee' (*Jer.* 7:16). God had declared that judgment must come, and that he would make Jerusalem desolate as Shiloh. All these are cases of judgment in this life, and do not speak of spiritual death.

[1] In a great many MSS. the reading is in danger of 'eternal *sin*' (*Mark* 3:29).

Second. The sin in our passage seems to be a sin *which the person is understood to be quite aware of.* Christ does not speak of it as mysterious. Yet we find most of those who fancy that they have committed the unpardonable sin cannot tell *what* it is, or *when,* or *how,* they were drawn into it. In most of such persons an indefinite fear or dread is all that can be detected as producing their misery; no positive deed or provocation has occurred, or is alleged; they do not point to any definite act.

Dr Spencer (*Sketches*) gives details of a case of this kind. One of his congregation used, from time to time, to spread her hopeless state before him, insisting that she must have committed *the unpardonable sin.* He pressed her to say what the sin was; she replied, 'Speaking against the Holy Ghost'; but when further asked, 'Have you been speaking against the Holy Ghost?' she said most earnestly, 'Oh, no! I have not done that.' On being pressed to state if she still fancied she had committed this sin, her reply was, 'God would have forgiven me before this time if it had not been for this sin.' Dr Spencer replied—'And so you think it is for no present fault of yours that you have not found acceptance, but for something done months ago?' 'Yes, sir.' Upon this he sent her away to tell her case to God; and when next day she persisted in repeating, 'I know I have committed that sin; I know I have! I know I have!' Dr Spencer firmly but kindly, and very plainly, showed her —(a) That it was *pride,* the foolish pride of a wicked heart, that made her speak thus, and led her to strive to believe that she had done this sin, that so she might be able to console herself with the thought that *some uncommon thing* was keeping her from salvation. (b) That she was *excessively self-righteous,* without perceiving it; trying to persuade herself that she was *not to blame for her unbelief,* for God was hindering her on account of this fancied sin. (c) That her gloomy fancy clung to the idea of this unpardonable sin as an *excuse for continuing in disobedience,* the hindrance all the time

45

being simply her wickedness of heart. She was looking away from her other sins and stifling all true conviction. The Lord blest this dealing; she saw that 'True light in the conscience is very different from a deceitful gloom in the proud heart.' She became alarmed at her desperately wicked heart, and her whole nature opposed to God and his Holy Law; and soon after found forgiveness, as other sinners do, in the blood of the Lamb.

Now many, by indulging some vague fancy such as this, torment themselves in vain. Let such persons carefully observe that Christ's words are plain, and lead to the conclusion that the person who speaks against the Holy Ghost *knows* that he has so done—knows that he has set himself directly and distinctly against the working of the Holy Ghost. If you do not know that you have so done, your very ignorance on this point is a proof that you have not fallen into the unpardonable sin.

Third. We have already shown what is the state of mind presented by one who has been guilty of this 'blasphemy', this insulting speaking against the Holy Ghost. We have seen that this sin induces a state of mind that inclines the person to seek out reasons which may justify him in rejecting Christ. It puts him in full opposition to Christ, and cold alienation from God; desire for fellowship is gone.

Never think, then, that you have committed this sin, if you are still under anxiety and concern about Christ. For in all cases of the unpardonable sin, *the sinning one loses all desires for Christ and salvation;* the Holy Spirit withdrawing altogether from the soul and leaving it to its own lusts and desires. One who knew much of soul-exercise has given it as his full and unhesitating conviction that, 'No soul is guilty of this unpardonable sin who believeth that Christ is the Son of God, and the Redeemer of the world, and who would fain have part in the merits and mercy of that Redeemer' (Richard Baxter in a sermon on this sin, III:23, 24.) He goes on to say,

The sin against the Holy Ghost casts out this desire. It is the sin of infidels, or at least of men that would have none of Christ if they might. Those, therefore, who would have Christ and yet fear they have committed this sin, they know not what they are afraid of; they know not what it is. It is a sign that a man hath not committed this sin against the Holy Ghost, when he is troubled with fear lest he hath committed it, and complaineth of his danger and sad condition.

To the same effect the eminent Archbishop Usher, in one of his sermons, asks, *'Why is that sin unpardonable?'* and his reply is, 'Only because it is the nature of the disease that it will not suffer the plaster to stick on. If this sinner would not tread the plaster under foot, he should be saved.'[1]

You may have committed some terrible crime; you may have given way to some outrageous and malignant display of defiance; you may be stained with foul guilt; you may have sinned against light and love. But so did Adam, who ruined millions upon millions by his sin, covering his own soul with appalling blackness: and yet to him was 'The Seed of the woman' freely given. So did Lot, after most remarkable deliverance, committing enormous wickedness, the very mention of which makes us shudder; yet he too found pardon, and is declared 'righteous' (*2 Pet.* 2:7). So was it with Saul of Tarsus, who hated Christ with a virulence and malignant intensity that had no parallel. Would you, then, fain go to the mercy-seat; go at once, for that desire is the Spirit's call to you. Go to the blood that cleanses, and assuredly you shall find welcome. It is for such as you; for if Christ sent the message, 'Tell my brethren, and Peter', selecting Peter because he was most likely to think himself excepted because of his denial, as truly is he sending a

[1] Dr Owen (*Mortification of Sin*, chap. 16) says of this sin, 'A man, by it is brought to renounce the means of his coming to the enjoyment of God.' 'He chooses to have no more to do with God.'

message to you in terms that surely take you in, 'Come unto me, *all* ye that labour and are heavy laden.' 'Let him that is athirst come, and *whosoever will*'.

Fourth. You surely do not give place to the idea that the Holy Ghost is more easily offended, and resents offence more readily, than the Father or the Son? You forget that the voice that shall say to the sinner, 'Thou shalt not enter into my rest', is the voice of the Godhead, the Father, the Son, and the Holy Ghost alike. Has some (almost sentimental) fancy about the Spirit being 'the Dove', and the Dove being very easily affrighted and driven away, made you suppose that the Spirit is far more likely to give you up soon, than Jesus the Saviour? Is he sensitive and touchy, after the manner of men? No; he is long-suffering and very pitiful. He is in all things, and to the same degree, as patient with us as Jesus has ever been; for his name is 'that *other Comforter*', the representative of Christ, the same in nature, the same in love and tenderness, dwelling in that believer's soul, just as Jesus dwelt in Nazareth; from day to day working there, in spite of all the evil that he witnesses. O blessed Spirit, how infinitely loving art thou! How slow to wrath! Mighty to save and infinitely able!

Fifth. Let us look back to the circumstance in which this passage was spoken. Let us look round upon the company of the 'Scribes from Jerusalem' and Pharisees that filled that room in the house at Capernaum. Just as Jesus had finished his solemn warning to them, some movement was heard at the door of the room, and a voice whispered to the Master that his mother and brethren were anxious to get admittance into the house (from which they had been shut out during this interview), desiring to see him. Jesus, ever kind and obedient to his mother, and ready to gratify every natural and lawful request of his brothers and sisters, seems at once to have prepared to comply with their desire: but before dismissing these Scribes and Pharisees spoke to them a most gracious word. In the *audience of these Scribes from Jerusalem and Pharisees who had been so malignant in their reviling, and had gone so near to the unpardonable sin,* he lifted up his voice, and pointing with his hand to his disciples, said, 'Who is my mother, and who are my brethren?' Every eye was again fixed, and every ear attentive, when he answered his own question. *'Whosoever shall do the will of my Father in heaven, the same is my brother, and sister, and mother.'* I am ready at this moment to take such to my heart, and to show myself as loving as I am to my mother, as considerate and sympathizing as I am to my brothers and sisters. To all such as *do the will of my Father!* To you, O Scribes and Pharisees, among the rest, in spite of all your blasphemies! Only *'Do the will of my Father'* by accepting me whom the Father has sent. For the way to 'do his will' (as written in *John* 6:29), is to see the Son and believe on him.' Yes, I say 'whosoever' of you, notwithstanding all your provocations, and blasphemies, and sins! 'whosoever' of you! The kingdom of heaven is come nigh unto you, and the door is open still.'

Jesus was truly man, 'Son of Man', and showed himself to be so in all his ways. When this interview was over, it appears, he left the heated room to go forth to the open air—*'He went out of the house and sat by the sea-side' (Matt.* 13:1), to be refreshed by the pleasant breeze and the quiet of the scene, pondering all the while what might be the effect of the words he had just spoken; for he had, with quick eye, perceived on the faces of his audience the different impressions made on different individuals. When thus engaged, 'that same day' (*Matt.* 13:1), he was noticed by the people, and soon a multitude of them pressed around him, thronging him, so that he got into a boat, and sat in it, while they lined the shore. Full of the subject that had occupied his thoughts, he opened his mouth and taught them the ever-memorable *'Parable of the Sower'*. He had been that day sowing seed; was it likely to spring up? There were many hindrances; let everyone look well to himself. 'Hearken!'

(*Matt.* 13:3). 'He that hath ears to hear, let him hear' (verse 9). Hear and be warned. Hear and be at rest!

7

WHAT GIVES ASSURANCE

Many are the persons who have envied Isaiah, to whom personally the messenger from the throne said, 'Thine iniquity is taken away, and thy sin is purged' (*Isa.* 6:7). They are ready to say, 'Oh, if we heard the same.' Many are the persons who have envied Daniel, to whom the Lord said, 'Thou shalt rest, and stand in thy lot at the end of the days' (*Dan.* 12:13). Daniel was thus assured of the future; with him it was to be at rest at death, and a lot, or portion (*Josh.* 15:1; 16:1), in the inheritance of the saints on the morning of the resurrection of the just. And so also have such persons wished that their case were that of the man to whom, directly and personally, Jesus said, 'Son, thy sins are forgiven thee' (*Mark* 2:5); or that of the woman in Simon's house, whose ear heard the blessed declaration, 'Thy sins are forgiven' (*Luke* 7:48); or even that of the thief, 'Today thou shalt be with me in paradise' (*Luke* 23:43). These sinners were all of them personally certified of pardon and acceptance, and we are ready to think that it would be the height of happiness for ourselves to have, like them, a declaration of our personal forgiveness sounding in our ear. Now, ere we have finished our subject, we may be able (if the Lord, the Spirit, lead us into the truth set forth in the Word) to see that, after all, we may be as sure and certain of our pardon and acceptance as any or all of these— as sure as Isaiah, Daniel, the palsied man, the woman sinner, the dying thief, and, let us add, as sure of it as Paul was of Clement and other fellow-labourers having their names in the Book of Life (*Phil.* 4:3). Nay, we may even discover that our certainty is in all respects higher than theirs was, being founded on something far better than one single announcement, which, in the lapse of time, might lose very much of its distinctness, and of its power.

Oh, how blessed to be able to point heavenward and say, 'It is mine!'—to point to the throne and say, 'He is mine who sitteth there!'—to look back and find your name in the Book of Everlasting love!—to look forward to the opening of the Book of Life, knowing that your name is in it!—to be able to anticipate resurrection, and to sing

> I know that safe with Him remains,
> Protected by His power,
> What I've committed to His trust
> Till the decisive hour.
>
> Then will He own His servant's name
> Before His Father's face,
> And in the New Jerusalem
> Appoint my soul a place.

We begin by noticing that *Assurance is far oftener spoken of than sought for.* Many may be said, in a vague sense, to wish for it, who after all do not seek after it. Not a few of our communicants, men of knowledge and good attainment, men of high Christian profession, are rather disposed to evade the question, Are you sure of your salvation? They are content to go on in uncertainty. Some of these even spurn from them the suggestion of any one having *full Assurance,* branding the idea as *Presumption.* They quite mistake the meaning of *Presumption,* which is claiming what we have not been invited to, and are not warranted to take. They do not see that there can be no presumption in our taking whatever our God has invited us to accept; and that, on the other hand, if we decline taking what our God presents to us, we are assuming to ourselves a right to judge of the fitness and wisdom of his proceedings.

Such persons are not in right earnest about salvation and the favour of God. They take things easy. They admit that they may die today or tomorrow, and that they do not certainly know what is to become of them; and yet they are making no effort to ascertain. They admit that the favour of God is the soul's real portion, and that they, as yet, cannot speak of that being their possession and enjoyment; and yet they coolly go on day after day without anxious inquiry regarding it.

There are others who, from a wrong religious training, go on in a sort of doubt and fear, cherishing the idea that these doubts and fears are salutary checks to pride, and that they are, on the whole, as safe with the *hope* that all is right, as they would be with the *certainty*. We generally find that these persons are misled by confounding things that differ. They perhaps quote to you, 'Happy is the man that feareth always' (*Prov.* 28:14), not perceiving that the *fear* there is the *'fear of the Lord'*, in which there is *'strong confidence'* (*Prov.* 14:26). Or, perhaps, they quote the unhappy experience of some godly men who died without speaking anything about assurance—not knowing that those godly men longed for certainty, and reckoned it so desirable that their very estimate of its preciousness made them jealous of admitting that they themselves might be partakers thereof.

But the truth is, in too many cases, these persons do not care for the close fellowship of God into which Assurance leads the soul. They do not wish to bask in the beams of divine love. They wish merely to be safe at last. But if you would see how entirely different is the effect of a merely hoped for impunity, from that of certainty in regard to divine favour, read these two passages, Deuteronomy 29:19, and 1 John 3:3. In the former case the sinner says, 'I shall have peace though I walk in the imagination of mine heart, to add drunkenness to thirst'; in the latter he says, 'Every man that hath this hope in him purifieth himself, even as he is pure."[1]

Once more, then, on this point let us ask attention to the fact that in the *New Testament* we have no encouragement given to doubts and uncertainties. The believers there are spoken of continually as having the joy of knowing the Saviour as theirs. No doubt there were in those days some believers who were not fully assured; but these were not meant to be any rule to us now that the Sun of Righteousness has risen so gloriously; and accordingly, no notice is taken of their case. On the other hand, we are ever meeting with such words as these spoken in the name of all disciples, *'We know* that if our earthly house of this tabernacle were dissolved, we have a building of God' (*2 Cor.* 5:1). *'We know* that we have passed from death unto life. *We know* that we are of God' (*1 John* 3:14; 5:19). *'I know* whom I have believed' (*2 Tim.* 1:12).[2]

---

[1] Let it be observed that in the New Testament the grace of hope does not imply doubt, but signifies the *expectation of the things which are yet future*. Hence the hope in 1 John 3:3, was thus stated in verse 2. *'We know* that when he shall appear we shall be like him.' Old writers used to quote a Latin saying, 'Hope, as used of earthly things, is a word for a good that is uncertain; hope, as used of heavenly things, is a word for good that is most sure.'

[2] The late Dr Sievewright, of Markinch, in a sermon upon *Eph.* 1:13, has remarked:—'In those primitive times, an apostle could take for granted of a whole church that they all trusted. For, in writing to the Ephesians, does Paul make a *single allusion to their unbelief?* Or, does he employ a single exhortation in the way of persuasion to believe? Or, from beginning to end of his Epistle, does he hint at such a thing as prevailing distrust? No; in those days Christian men no more thought of refusing to trust in the Saviour, than of denying the Word of Truth. But now, is it not a frequent case that a man shall go by a Christian name and practise Christian duties, and receive Christian privileges, for years together, while he is so far from trusting in Christ with the confidence of faith, that he shall not only confess himself destitute of truth, but often express a fear lest full trust and confidence were an unwarranted and dangerous presumption? *How strange this would have sounded in the apostles' time,* when to trust in Christ, and to trust fully and for all salvation, *was the very first exercise* to which they called those who

But it is time to speak of *what gives Assurance*. Of course, we understand that this blessing, like the other blessings of salvation, every one, is the free gift of a sovereign God. It is the 'God of hope' who gives it 'through the power of the Holy Ghost' (*Rom.* 15:13). But our present point of inquiry is, In what way does it please him to give it to souls? All agree that Christ's person and work furnish the materials and groundwork of a sinner's acceptance, peace, assurance. 'Peace' (says *Isa.* 32:17) 'is the fabric reared by righteousness; yea, the office of righteousness is to give quietness and assurance for ever.' But there is a difference of opinion and practice as to the way of using these ample materials. We begin with speaking of what we may call,

First, THE INDIRECT, OR LONG WAY.

Those who try this way set themselves to ascertain *'What am I?'* They seek to make sure that they have the marks and evidences of being new creatures in Christ, or at least the marks and evidences of having, beyond doubt, believed in him. Divines have been wont to call this mode of Assurance *'the Assurance of sense'*, because in it the person points to sensible proofs of his new nature, and thinks he may some time or other be able to show such an experience of divine things, as puts it beyond doubt that he has believed and has found Christ. It is quite wrong, however, to apply the Scriptural term, *'Assurance of hope'*, to this experimental sort of certainty; for Scripture means the assured belief and expectation of things yet future, by that expression. We may call it, for clearness' sake, *Assurance got by seeing effects produced*. Divines often describe it as *Assurance derived from the reflex acts of the soul.*

(a) One form which the pursuit of Assurance in the long, or indirect, way takes is this,—it leads the person to put much stress

---

were awakened to seek in earnest for eternal life, and receive the record of God concerning the way. The remarkable trust of the first Christians gave a perfection to their character we now seldom perceive.'

on his *own act of believing*. In this case the person, being much
concerned about his state towards God, and fearful of mistaking
the matter, says to himself, 'I know that all assurance of salvation
depends on my believing in Christ, and I think I believe; but what
if I be deceiving myself as to my supposed believing?' Haunted
by this thought, he sets himself to remedy the danger by trying
to convince himself that he has believed. And in order to make
himself sure that he has faith, he resolves not to be satisfied till he
sees the full fruits of faith. He puts such stress on his own act of
believing, that he will not be content until he sees, by such effects
as hypocrites could not imitate, that his is and has all along been
genuine faith.

Now, we say to such—*You are not taking the best way to have real
fruit;* for you are seeking fruit and effects from a selfish motive;
you are not seeking holiness as an end, and for its own sake, but
in order to use it as an evidence in favour of your sincerity. This
kind of fruit is not likely to be the best, nor the most satisfac-
tory. We say again—*You are putting Assurance far off.* It can only
be at some distant future day that you arrive at any certainty by
your method; for such fruits as you seek cannot be visible very
soon. But we say again—*You are by this method taking off your eye
from Christ, to a great degree.* For you try to believe, and then you
look into yourself to see if you have believed. You look up to the
Brazen Serpent, and then you take off your eye to examine your
wound, and to see if the bites are really healing, that so you may
be sure you have looked aright! Would a bitten Israelite have put
such stress on his own poor act of looking? You are looking at
Christ, and then looking away from him to yourself. You are like
a gardener who, after planting a tree or flower in rich soil, might
be foolish enough to uncover the soil in order to see if the root
had struck, and was really imbibing the moisture. Surely, better
far to let the root alone, having once ascertained the richness of

the soil, and allow the plant to spread out its leaves to the warmth of the sun. Keep looking on Christ, and the effects cannot fail to follow.

(b) Another form that this same indirect method takes is somewhat similar. Those who adopt it do not expect Assurance at the outset, and say that it is presumption and pride in young believers to speak of being sure of their interest in Christ; for where is there time for them to have experience, or exhibit fruits? Such persons think that ripe, mature fruits of holiness alone entitle any one to say, 'I know that I am in Christ.' If we might so speak, they do not allow the newly engrafted branch (though really engrafted by the Heavenly Husbandman) to say, 'I am in the vine'—no, they say, wait till you have borne fruit, and then when the clusters appear on your boughs, you may be entitled to say, 'I am in the vine.' But not till then.

It is a favourite argument with such that, in 1 John 3:14, the Apostle John says, *'We* know that we have passed from death unto life, *because we love the brethren';* but this does not prove that this is *the only way* of knowing that we are passed from death unto life. It only shows that an aged and experienced saint, like John, thought it good sometimes to bring forward his own and his fellow-believers' brotherly love as a marked and unmistakable feature of their Christian character. It is very much as if he had said, 'We believers know each other, as having passed from death unto life, by the love that fills our hearts toward each other.' He is not speaking to the question, 'Is this the first, or is it the only trustworthy way, by which you know your interest in Christ? Surely, so far from this being the case, John would at once have said that he himself found rest in knowing *the love of him who begat,* before he discerned in himself any love to those begotten of him.

The truth is, this long and indirect way is properly the way by which others ascertain your standing in Christ. But there is another way for the person's self, of which we are yet to speak. Also; this way is good even for the person's self as confirmatory of the short and direct way, of which we are yet to speak. But still we say, if it were the only way, then farewell to gospel-joy, except in the very rarest cases. For the more a soul grows in grace, the more that the believing man rests in Christ and drinks into his Spirit, just the more dissatisfied does he become with all his fruits; his holiness does not please him; he finds defects in it; he finds it mixed and impure; and the longer he lives the life of faith, he gets more and more keen-sighted in detecting blemishes in his graces.[1] So that it is difficult indeed to say when a growing believer, ever jealous of himself, and his conscience becoming more and more tender, will accumulate such a heap of this gold, such an amount of really holy living, as will put beyond doubt, to his own mind, that he is a man between whom and Christ there exists the bond of union. If good works or holiness must be waited for ere faith can be known to be genuine, when are we to expect to attain to an amount or quality sufficiently satisfying?

If this were the only way of Assurance, we could not wonder that many should speak of it as necessarily a very rare attainment, and even as all but impossible. This, however, is not the only way; and we now turn from this way to the other, quoting, as we turn to it, the statement of the old Puritan writer, Thomas Brooks:—

'Many of God's dear people are so taken up with their own hearts and duties, and graces, that Christ is little regarded by them, or minded; and what is this but to be more taken up with the streams than with the fountain? with the bracelets, and earrings,

---

[1] John Newton, in his sermon, 'Of the Assurance of Faith', remarks—'If inherent sanctification, or a considerable increase of it, be considered as the proper ground of Assurance, those who are most humble, sincere, and desirous of being conformed to the will of God, will be the most perplexed and discouraged in their search after it. For they, of all others, will be the least satisfied with themselves, and have the quickest sense of innumerable defilements.'

and gold chains, than with the husband? with the nobles than with the king?"[1] And then he adds, 'Dear Christian, was it *Christ,* or was it your graces, gracious evidences, gracious dispositions, gracious actings, that trod the wine-press of the Father's wrath?' And once more:—'These persons forget their grand work, which is *immediate* closing with Christ, *immediate* embracing of Christ, *immediate* relying , resting, staying upon Christ.'

Let us turn then, to the *Second,* THE DIRECT OR SHORT WAY.

They who take this way, set themselves to ascertain *'Who and what Christ is.'* The Holy Spirit, we believe, delights very specially to use this way, because it turns the eye of the sinner so completely away from self to the Saviour.

What we call the *direct and short way,* is that in which we are enabled by the Spirit at once to look up to Christ, the Brazen Serpent, and to be satisfied in looking on him. This simple, direct Assurance is got by what we discern in Christ himself; not by what we discover about ourselves. It is got by what we believe about Christ; not by what we know about our own act of faith. We may (like 'Poor Joseph')[2] know nothing about our own soul's actings in believing, and yet we may so know him on whom we believe as to find ourselves altogether at rest. In a word, this direct and immediate Assurance is found by my discovering that Christ, God-man, is the very Saviour for my needs and wants, my sins and corruptions; while all the time I may never be once troubled about the question, Am I sure that I believe, and that my act of faith possesses the right quality?

---

[1] Thomas Brooks, *Cabinet.*

[2] Some friends who came to see him wondered on hearing him always dwell on this, and this only, *Joseph is the chief of sinners, but Jesus came into the world to save sinners.'* They said, 'But what say you of your own heart, Joseph? Is there no token for good about it? Have you closed with Christ by acting faith upon him?' His reply was, 'Joseph can act nothing. Joseph has nothing to say about himself but that he is the chief of sinners; yet, since it is a faithful saying that Jesus came into the world to save sinners, why may not Joseph be saved?'

I find it when the Spirit is taking the things of Christ, and showing them to my soul; and I do not need to wait till he next shows me what is in me. Let us explain the matter more fully.

I have assurance that God accepts me *the moment I see the fullness and freeness of Christ's work*. My soul is enabled to see all the claims of justice satisfied at the cross; for there is completed obedience, there is the full penalty paid. At the cross there is room for any sinner, and the gospel invites me as a sinner among the rest to hear what the cross says. Does it not say to me, 'God-man has provided an infinitely perfect righteousness, and made it honourable for the holy God to embrace the Prodigal Son. Yonder, in the work of God-man, is a *rock* for the sinner's feet to stand upon—and this not a mere narrow point, hardly sufficient, but rather a wide continent, stretching out on every side. Surely there is room for me there? I feel it is enough!' Self is forgotten in presence of this marvellous scene. What could satisfy the conscience better? What could speak peace like this? This is faith rising to Assurance while simply continuing to behold its glorious object.

And then, if any one try to disturb me by the suggestion, 'How do you know that you are really believing what you recognise as so suited to your need?'—my reply is simply this, 'How do I know that I see the sun when I am in the act of gazing upon him in the splendour of his setting?' That glowing sky, and that globe of mild but ineffable glory cannot be mistaken, if anything is sure to the human vision.

The believer's own consciousness[1] (quickened of course by the Spirit) is sufficient, in presence of the cross, to assure him that he, a sinner, is most certainly welcome to the bosom of the Holy

---

[1] Rutherford, in a sermon on Luke 8:22, says, 'When I believe in Christ, that instinct of the grace of God, stirred up by the Spirit of God, maketh me know that I know God, and that I believe, and so that I am in Christ, to my own certain apprehension.' He then adds, that 'this does not hinder other inferior evidences.'

One, who, pointing to the 'It is finished', cries, 'Return to me, for I have redeemed thee.' Just look at it again. Your soul hears that the Father is well pleased with the full atonement of the Lord Jesus Christ, his Son. He condemns and rejects all your works, all your efforts, and your guilty person! but when you turn to his Son, our Substitute, his obedience and his suffering unto death are found most glorifying to the Holy One and his holy law. And while you are pondering the Father's delighted rest in Christ, who thus wrought all for us, your soul is 'like the chariots of Amminadab' (*Song of Sol.* 6:12); in a moment, you feel your conscience has got rest, as if a voice from that atoning work had said, 'Peace, be still.' Your sins, placed in God's balance, were outweighed by Christ's infinite merit; and, if so, your sins in your own balance are no less surely outweighed by the same weight of immense merit. What satisfies God, satisfies you.

Thus faith, as it gazes on its object, passes on to full Assurance. And if now, again, anyone seek to disturb your calm rest by asking, 'Are you quite sure that you do really believe what is giving you such rest?'—what other reply could you give but this, 'As well ask me, when I am enjoying and revelling in the glories of the setting sun, Are you sure your eye really sees that sun which you so admire?'

I sit down and meditate on such a passage as John 3:16, 'God so loved the world, that he gave his only begotten Son, that whosoever believeth in him should not perish, but have everlasting life.' The Spirit enables me to see in these words that God is testifying that no more is needed for my acceptance with God than what is found in Christ: and that all that Christ has done becomes mine upon believing in him. Relying on God's testimony, I ask no questions, I wait for nothing in myself (such as love, sorrow, or other feeling), but I think on what is in Christ, as the ground of my peace. And when I so muse, the fire burns—my soul is at rest.[1] And

---

[1] Halyburton (*Mem.* chap. 2, p. 3) says, 'A sweet and comfortable hope and

if, now, any one disturbs, or threatens to disturb, my calm enjoyment of my Father's love by hinting, 'You should first, ere ever you venture to rest, be sure that you are really believing the things that are making you so glad';—my reply to such an unseasonable interruption might be somewhat in the style of a writer who uses the following illustration. Suppose a nobleman condemned for high treason, and the day has come when he must die. But that morning, a document is put into his hand; it is a pardon from the king, on no other terms than that he accept it. He reads; as he reads, his countenance is flushed, his eye glistens, and in a moment he is full of joy. What think you of any one arresting the current of his joy by the suggestion, 'Are you quite sure you are accepting of the pardon? Is your act of repentance complete and thorough?' No; the man is engrossed with the certainties presented to his thoughts, viz., what the king freely gives to him; and these certainties convey their own impression to his soul,—to wit, the certainty of his pardon.

Such is the *direct way of Assurance*. We called it a short and an immediate way. Is it not so? We said, too, at the beginning, that it might turn out that, after all, we had a way of knowing our pardon and acceptance, superior in many respects to that by which on one occasion it was conveyed to Isaiah, and on another to Daniel, and on another to the palsied man, and to the woman-sinner, and to the thief. We still adhere to our statement. For our way of knowing our acceptance, you see, is one that rests on *unalterable facts*, the significance of which cannot pass away or decay. If it decay from our souls for a time, we can revive it again by a renewed study of the facts that produced it at the first. Whereas the one utterance that assured Isaiah, Daniel, and those others mentioned might, in process of time, be found to fade somewhat in its vividness; and

---

persuasion of my own salvation was answerable to the clearness of the discovery of the way of salvation. The hope rose in strength, or grew weak, as the discoveries of the way of salvation were more or less clear and strong.'

then the individual might say to himself, 'Ah, what if I have over-estimated the meaning of the utterance! or—what if I have forgot it in part? or what if my subsequent unworthiness have cancelled the promise?' In a dull, self-reproaching mood of mind, such a partial obliteration from the mind or memory of a single, solitary announcement is quite a possible occurrence; not to refer to other abatements, such as that the person in a case like Isaiah's might say to himself, 'What if it referred only to the past, but did not include what has happened since then?' But, on the other hand, our way of ascertaining our pardon and acceptance rests on unchanging and unchangeable facts,—facts for ever illustrious, facts for ever rich in meaning, facts forever uttering the same loud, distinct, full testimony to the sinner's soul. Yes, we have an altar, and the voice from that altar and its four horns may be heard distinctly from day to day at first hand. Our altar is Christ; and this Christ died, rose again, went back to the Father, is interceding for us. These are the four horns of our altar! Let us take hold of any one of them, and lo! we see an accepted sacrifice before us, a sacrifice that speaks peace, that leads our conscience to rest, and makes our hearts leap for joy; for God is well pleased. We have God's Word reiterating in manifold ways a testimony to be believed; and so we find security against Satan's whispered suspicions.

And should any one object, 'Surely there have been many, very many, good men and eminent men of God, who did not take this *short and direct way*;'—let us remind such as may stumble at this fact (for it is a fact) of an anecdote which good old Brooks[1] has recorded. A minister, who had great joy in Christ, said on his death-bed regarding his peace and quietness of soul, 'Thus he enjoyed these not from having *a greater measure of grace* than other Christians had, nor from any special immediate witness of the Spirit, but because he had *more clear understanding of the covenant of grace.*'

[1] *Cabinet*, p. 113.

O Spirit of truth, give all thy servants this clear understanding of the *covenant of grace!*

Nor must we fail to notice this immediate direct way is that which specially honours God and his beloved Son, inasmuch as it magnifies free grace. Here is the Lord's free love manifesting itself as so exceedingly free, that he will not ask the price of one moment's waiting or delay. Behold the cross, and at once be at rest! The excuses of the delaying sinner are swept away. Why wait, since all is ready! and where is there room for the plea that God's time for favour, and so great for favour as that of making you sure of acceptance, may not have come? God in Christ waits for you,[1] presenting and proffering to you an immediate welcome, immediate peace.

[1] It is a very common mistake to allege that God sometimes counsels us *to wait*. But, if *wait* be used in the sense of delay, or putting off immediate decision, we assert there is no passage in the Bible to countenance such an idea. Some quote *Psa.* 40:1, 'I *waited patiently* for the Lord', which is (see the margin) 'In waiting, I waited', or 'I eagerly waited.' Now not to insist on the fact that here the speaker is *Christ our surety*, we must remember that the Old Testament use of 'wait' has not in it anything of the idea of procrastination, or delay or *contented waiting* in our sense of the term. It always means *eager looking*, as when a dog looks up to his master's table for the crumbs, or as when the people waited for the priest coming out of the Holy Place, or as in *Job* 29:23, the anxious, intensely anxious, looking out for rain in sultry weather. This is the meaning, *Mic.* 7:7, 'I will wait for the God of my salvation.' This is the meaning, *Hab,* 2:3, 'Though it tarry, wait for it'; that is, if you do not see these things come to pass at once, if you do not see at once the Lord appear in his glory to overthrow his foes, yet look out for it anxiously! eagerly hasten on to that day. This is the way in which God's people 'wait', spoken of in *Psa.* 130:6; *Isa.* 40:31. And so *Lam.* 3:25 is the case of the desolate soul in affliction, earnestly looking up and looking out for deliverance, though calm and resigned. Scriptural waiting is not in the least like that of the careless, easy-minded soul, that pretends it is unwilling to anticipate sovereign grace. And when God himself, in *Isa.* 30:18, is said to 'wait to be gracious', the same idea of eager, earnest looking is implied. It is the intensely anxious waiting of the Prodigal's Father for the return of his son, for whose coming he is ever on the look-out. Most certainly, there is nothing in Scripture that countenances an unbelieving waiting for faith.

What say you then, *unassured soul?* Are you still content? Assurance may be got in beholding steadfastly the Lamb of God; and is there no sin in your refusing to behold him steadfastly? Want of Assurance leaves you in the awful position of being, on your own showing, possibly still a child of Satan! And can you remain thus without alarm? And the world is passing away. You are dying men. Christ is coming quickly, coming as a thief in the night, coming in an hour that you think not; and you are not ready to meet him at his coming. There are not less than 80,000 of our fellow men dying every day; 80,000 have died today, 80,000 more shall die tomorrow, and you may be one of that number whom the scythe of death shall cut down as grass—and yet you are content to have only a vague hope! Content to be without Assurance! You are like the unhappy philosopher who said, 'I have lived uncertain, I die doubtful, I know not whither I am going.' Are things to continue thus with you any longer? Do the visions of an eternal hell never rise up before you? Are you never struck with cold fear lest hell be waiting for you? Mirth is most unsuitable for you; laughter is out of season; peace cannot take up her abode under your roof, for you are all at sea about your eternal interests! Yes, you may be almost past all the joy that you are ever to find! Will you not now stand still, and once more examine Christ crucified, Christ's finished work, to see if that cannot yield you the present and eternal peace which alone can satisfy the soul? We have sought to set all before you; and now we leave you, praying that the Holy Spirit may give efficacy to our words, knowing well that otherwise all is vain.

> Let all the promises before Him stand,
> And set a Barnabas at His right hand.
> These in themselves no comfort can afford;
> 'Tis Christ, and none but Christ, can speak the word.

8

GREATER HOLINESS

For we know that the law is spiritual: but I am carnal, sold under
sin. For that which I do I allow not: for what I would, that do I
not; but what I hate, that do I.

Romans 7:14-25

The *personal holiness of believers is of immense importance.* The
strength of all the Epistles may be said to be directed to this
point. It is taken for granted, in all these Epistles, that, to attract
men to Christ, we must exhibit a Christlike walk; and experience
in every age proves that *'winning Christ' (Phil.* 3:8) makes us *win-*
ners of souls. Yet, how often is this overlooked. Many good men,
in their intense evangelistic zeal, seem to make light of growth in
grace, and will even be heard saying, when a soul has been apparently led to Christ, 'Oh, leave him now; all is right with him; let
us go on to others.' This is a grievous mistake. That may be a saved
soul; but he may, *by his imperfect holiness, prevent the conversion of*
twenty others. He is a lighthouse; but if the reflectors be dim, and
the supply of oil scanty, the dimness of the light may wreck many
a vessel which never doubted all was well, since no warning ray on
the waters gave notice of danger. Or, to take a scriptural thought;
if raised Lazarus had been left with his grave clothes unremoved,
the napkin on his face, and the smell of the tomb's corruption lingering in these cerements, would he not have repelled those who
came to him? Would he not have left on them the impression that

this specimen of the Saviour's resurrection-power might almost as well have been left in the tomb?

We must give most earnest and continual attention to our personal holiness and growth, even for the sake of winning others. I thought of this truth the other day, when a sailor was telling me that when far out at sea his captain, toward sunset, after seeing that all was right in the vessel, used to send one of the crew to the masttop, with instructions to use his glass, and look all round, lest some disabled vessel might be within sight. Each morning at sunrise the same survey was taken; for, his own vessel being all in order, he could afford to look out for others in need of help. In this way they were the means of bringing deliverance to not a few. Is not this a word in season to saints? Your own souls well cared for, you can and will, day by day, look out for souls whom you may bless—but you cannot afford to do so, if your own souls be not in order.

(1.) *But is it possible to be very holy in the midst of an evil world?* Our union to Christ, if we be saints at all, tells us that it is. Our union to Christ leaves us inexcusable for imperfect holiness; for Christ is *'our life'* (*Col.* 3:4); life for us is in him without limit.

But perhaps it has been the case in all ages, and certainly it is so now, that all saints do not attain to equal degrees of holiness. In the varieties of meat-offerings mentioned in Leviticus 2, this seems hinted at, the meat-offering being prepared in different forms, not so much (it may be) because of the comparative ability or inability of the offerer in regard to substance, as in regard to spiritual feeling. In David's host there were many warriors, all like each other; and then thirty outstanding ones; and then three who excelled all the rest. May there be something here for us? higher and lower degrees of attainment? Did our Lord intend to lead us on from a lower to a higher stage, and then to a still higher, when he used the words, *'Ask'*, *'seek'*, *'knock'*, as if to intimate that there would be found in his church those whose spiritual frames would correspond to these three words, the last being the highest, suggesting intense earnestness that will not be denied, but will knock loud and often, till every chamber of the house of David is opened to him? At all events, we have apparently a specific announcement of this difference in our Lord's words, in the parable of the Sower—'Other fell into good ground, and brought forth fruit, some an *hundred-fold,* some *sixty-fold,* some *thirty-fold*' (*Matt.* 13:8); or, as Mark 4:8 puts it, 'Some thirty, and some sixty, and some an hundred.'

Using this statement of our master, let us show how something answering to it may be seen very commonly among us. And let us, in so doing, make use of a well-known passage in the Epistle to the Romans, chap. 7:14-25. It may help us to see several things of importance in reference to different degrees of grace. Observe, then, that in the Church of Christ, among true and real believers—all of whom can say (*Rom.* 8:1), 'There is no condemnation to us who are in Christ'—there is nevertheless a difference of attainment in holiness (in some thirty, in some sixty, and in some an hundred-fold), which may be illustrated thus:—

(a) Romans 7:14-25 is the normal, or habitual experience of some believers. Are these not like the *'thirty-fold'*? They are ever complaining of broken resolutions, wandering thoughts, the power of corruption, the law in their members warring against the law of their mind, and dragging them into captivity. In them concupiscence, or desire for things of the flesh, is strong. They have little to say of victories; of 'peace keeping the heart and mind through Jesus Christ'; only they do get a glimpse of his grace in the midst of all their troubles: and if they cry, 'O wretched man that I am' (verse 24), they also cry, 'I thank God, through Jesus Christ our Lord' (verse 25). They can give thanks with one lately gone to glory, that 'when borne away by the power of indwelling sin they are only *prisoners of war,* not *deserters'.*

(b) Romans 7:14-25 is, from time to time, more or less, the experience of another class, but is not by any means their prevailing state. They may help us to illustrate the *'sixty-fold'*. They work cheerfully for God. They enjoy much fellowship with God, singing daily, 'Thine anger is turned away, and thou hast comforted us'; for their eye rests on Christ, in whom they see themselves at all times accepted by the Father. Still, their fellowship with God is frequently broken in upon. They feel the motions of sin, and desire for things of the flesh costs them many prayers and incessant watching. They are made to cry, 'There is a law in my members dragging me into captivity.' But they are not overcome. While, with David Brainerd, they are forced to cry, 'O that my soul were holy as God is holy; must I be sinning so long as I am in this world!' or, with Romans 7:24, 'O wretched man that I am, who shall deliver me out of the body of this death',—they are habitually able to recover the tone of triumph, 'I thank God, through Jesus Christ our Lord!'

(c) In the case of the *'hundred-fold'*, the victory over indwelling sin is more decided; and obvious to others, if not to themselves also. The solicitations of the flesh and Satan's temptations by means of the flesh and the world, are watched against and baffled by the soul being enabled to *'abide in Christ'* habitually and consciously, enjoying wonderful communion with the Lord, and enabled to live for him from day to day, in all manner of service. Yet even these may be heard telling the Lord of 'the law of sin in their members, which would fain drag them into captivity'; and they become of very quick discernment in regard to their corruptions and failures, their omissions and neglects.

Such is a general delineation of what may be supposed to be indicated by the thirty, sixty, and hundred-fold.

(2.) But some maintain that there are saints (of *this hundred-fold class*) who get entire victory over indwelling sin, and are not troubled with the conflict spoken of in Romans 7:14-25 any longer. One goes the length of saying, 'You may so get into contact with Jesus, that holiness will be yours; power, such supernatural power, peace, and gladness, as circumstances will no more affect than a summer breeze affects Mount Blanc.' But surely no passage of Scripture authorizes us to expect such attainment as this; though it may be said we are allowed to aim at it, because of the fullness of life for us in Christ. Paul was not superior to the influence of circumstances; holy as he was, he had not attained, even after being in the third heavens, what is described above. For in 2 Corinthians 2:12, 13, he tells us he was so affected by the circumstance of Titus not arriving at Troas, that he had no rest in his spirit, and was so unhinged that he could not embrace the opportunity he had of preaching the gospel.

It is often asked, whether or not, on to his last hour, Paul would have occasion to use his own words (*Rom.* 7:14-25) as his own experience. It may have been so, or it may have not. That passage does not decide the matter; for the drift of it is not so much to *describe* the conflict that goes on within us by reason of indwelling sin, as to *explain* it. That conflict is a phenomenon in the new creation that needs explanation; and Paul is taught of the Holy Ghost to give it. It is to this effect.

Having fully set forth justification by faith in Jesus, he had also shown the *privileges* that follow (chap. 5); thereafter, the *holiness* it entails (chap. 6; 7:1-6); and then *our relation to the law*. On this last point, having shown that we are not under the law as a covenant of works, being completely freed from all its charges against us, it might appear as if he were disparaging God's law. Accordingly, he takes great pains to show the excellency of the law (7:7, onward). And here our passage comes in. He wishes to make plain to us that the law does not lead to sin, and that the new nature in us quite agrees with the law. The law is an exhibition of God's mind and will; the new nature cannot disown it. 'The law is holy, and every precept of it holy, and just and good' (verse 12). It is a miserable mistake in some good men to speak disparagingly of the law of God; they might as well speak slightingly of his holy will and loving heart. *'We know* [says the apostle, at verse 14, using what is his favourite phraseology when speaking of the universally acknowledged verities] that the *law is spiritual';* i.e., it teaches the mind of the Spirit; the mind of the Holy Ghost; the mind, therefore, and heart, and will of God. Thus, with unqualified satisfaction, he exalts the law. How is it, then, that a man justified and saved commits sin? Is sin his element? The reply is, *'I am carnal, when I am sold under sin',* i.e., I breathe the mind of the flesh, my old nature, when at any time I have been hurried into sin. He takes for granted that any justified person may be borne away by sin within him. He uses the expression *'sold',* to show that for the time he has been carried off like a captive, or kidnapped; and in the original he uses a participle (πεπραμενος) which speaks of the things *having been done by another.* At such time (he says) I am manifesting the mind of the flesh. For the thing which I at such a time carry out into act, I disallow; for I do not (at such a time) set myself energetically to perform the thing as if I wished it; it is a thing I hate that I am found doing. So that I consent to the law that it is good (excellent), in the very act of doing what I do not wish; and it is not that [properly] I do it, but sin still dwelling in me (verses 14, 16, 17): for I know that in my flesh, my old nature, *good* (see verse 13) does not dwell. For (let me repeat it), a desire to do what is right is in me, even when I fail. It is true I perform not the good I desired, but on the contrary, do the evil that I did not desire; still, inasmuch as I do not desire it, it is not I (the justified man in Christ) that do it, but indwelling sin. The sum of the matter, therefore, is this: I find at such times a law of evil present with me, though I desire to do what is right; I say, a law of evil, not the new nature at work. For I delight in the law of God ('after the inner man') in my inmost soul, with my whole heart (*Eph.* 3:16); but I see another law in my members, warring against the divine law which my mind approves, and seeking to drag me into captivity, and make me a slave to the law of sin, which is in my members. My cries at such times are, 'O wretched man, who shall deliver me out of the body of this death? I thank God through Jesus Christ our Lord.' So that you see I, my true self, am a bondman (δουλευω)[1] to the law of God, so much do I love it and honour it! It is only my flesh (the old nature, not the new) that loves the law of sin.

You see now the drift of Paul's argument there. He is not undertaking to state his own experience farther than to explain that when, at any period after his justification, whether in his quarrel with Barnabas (*Acts* 15:39), or in his despondency at Troas (*2 Cor.* 2:12, 13), sin appeared at work; it is not the fruit of the new nature, it is not the genuine result of freedom from the bondage of the old covenant. No! the justified man loves the law of God, delights in it, in his inner man; for the truth is, if he be like Christ, that 'law is within his heart' (*Psa.* 40:8). If he be a partaker of the blessings of the new covenant, God has 'put his laws into his mind, and written them on his heart' (*Heb.* 8:10). Love to God, kindled at God's love to him, is, the *motive-power;* and the holy, just, good law of God is ever his blessed rule. It is 'the highway of holiness'.

(3.) But now we come back to the question of *how far we may attain in holiness?* We may surely say that we are warranted, nay; called upon, to aim at the *hundred-fold*. We have dwelt on Paul's case, because some try hard to make out that such was not his experience as a justified man, fancying that if it were, it might be quoted in favour of contentment with very imperfect holiness. Now the plain, obvious, unforced meaning of the passage is totally in contradiction to their view. At the same time, we are alive to the

[1] The very same word is used in the Greek version of Exodus 21:6, when telling of the servant whose ear was bored to the door-post, that he might thereby express his hearty love to his master, and his delight in his service.

fact that many do abuse the passage, making it an excuse for their unvanquished indwelling sin; and so we wish to state again, that there is nothing in the passage to forbid our believing that Paul was not speaking of this state of conflict as habitual. If a physician carefully expounds the relation of a patient's wounds and bruises to health, we cannot infer that he meant thereby to inform us that the patient was always smarting under sore wounds. At all events, we must not, on any account, use Romans 7:14-25 to excuse ourselves for a low degree of grace, a thirty-fold, when we might have had an hundred. If some have gone to what seem great extremes in maintaining the possibility of 'reaching heights of holiness, where no breeze of earth can affect them'; let us, at any rate, press up higher than we have done.

Very possibly, some of those who seem to claim for themselves an attainment that looks like perfection, mean rather a state in which *they are not at the moment conscious of sin*. This may be all they mean; absorbed in the love of God and his fellowship, they, for the time, feel nothing of earth or of sin. Of course, this is *not perfection*. Our consciousness does not prove much. A man may not be conscious to himself of sin, and yet may be far from 'loving God with ALL his heart, and ALL his soul, and ALL his mind, and ALL his strength', which is the only real perfection, and not to be reached till Christ come. 'When we shall see him we shall be like him' (*1 John* 3:2).

But (we say) let us not be deterred by the extreme statements of some men from aiming very high. Let us take a case of high attainment, the details of which are recorded with most minute particularity, and in all soberness of style. The case is that of the wife of Jonathan Edwards, related by himself in his published work on the great revival at Northampton. She was apparently converted at five years of age, and at the age of thirteen was noticed by all her friends as one living near God, often enjoying seasons of inexpressible delight in meditation and prayer. In 1728, at the time of her marriage (she was in her eighteenth year), friends spoke of her as having made singular progress in holiness: but this was only the beginning of her attainments. This was her period of 'lower degrees of grace'. She was subject to unsteadiness in her frames, her temperament being rather of a melancholy cast. But divine grace overcame these disadvantages. In 1738, after a new resignation of herself to the Lord, she found her views of the glory of God, and the excellency of Christ, become wonderfully enlarged. 'A kind of omnipotent joy' filled her heart, and she lived from day to day in 'all the riches of full assurance', says her husband. She had wonderful access to God in prayer; it often seemed to her that Christ was as near as if he was on earth standing by. She never felt any inclination, on this account, to slight the means of grace, but rather more and more prized them as most needful to her soul's growth. She used to look forward to the Sabbath with great desire, and began on Saturday her preparation for it. Several times after this, she anew dedicated herself to the Lord, renouncing self and the world, and seeking 'life more abundantly'. In 1742, one day, having had her usual calm of mind disturbed by some things that bore on her husband's concerns and her own good name, she saw she must ask yet more from the Lord, that she might be enabled to resign herself more entirely still to him. The words of Romans 8:33 to the end, 'Who shall lay anything to the charge of God's lect? Who shall separate us from the love of Christ?' etc., were brought home to her with extraordinary power, and seemed to tell her of God's unchangeableness, and her own unchangeable security in him, so certainly that 'the everlasting mountains and hills were but shadows in comparison.' At the same time, Christ was seen to be a mighty Saviour, 'The Lion of the tribe of Judah, *taking her heart with all its corruptions under his care, and putting all under his feet.*' Not that she fancied herself free from sin, for she was even led to perceive more fully the sinfulness of her heart. And thus she was enabled to go on from day to day, week to week, year to year, as testified by such a calm, credible witness as President Edwards, who watched and wondered at her walk during the remaining eight years they were spared to each other.

All the while there was no apparent tendency to pride, but rather deep abasement of soul, through a continual sense of unworthiness; a willingness to go behind all who were going heavenward. Her compassion for the lost and perishing often took away her rest; she was full of love to mankind. Her husband persuaded her to put down something of her feelings in writing for his own use; and among other things she says: 'My heart and soul flowed out in love to Christ; there seemed a constant flowing and reflowing of heavenly and divine love from Christ's heart to mine.' And all this did not weaken, but, on the contrary, it greatly strengthened her daily attention to ordinary, commonplace duties. 'I realized how great a part of godliness lies in the performance of our social and relative duties to one another.' Necessary *worldly business* was found by her *'as good as prayer when done as service to God'*. She made her husband's home the abode of neatness and order, peace and domestic comfort; sparing no pains to have everything in family arrangements pleasant and agreeable to the family, and to visitors. She was never gloomy, but always cheerful, even under sickness; guests and visitors found her most pleasant and kind. She bestowed great care on all her children's training; was tender, but very firm in exacting obedience; and failed not to discipline them to good habits in all departments. She would, for example, inculcate the duty of watching against wastefulness and carelessness, often reminding her children 'that Christ bade his disciples gather up the fragments of that bread which he had just before so easily created by a word.' She was free from all censoriousness: saying as little as possible about other people's imperfections. Withal, she was liberal in giving away, and very charitable to the poor. It was always when her health was best and her mind most vigorous that her enjoyments were highest.

One other remarkable feature in her high attainment of holiness must not be omitted. She had oftentimes an extraordinary view of the infinite terribleness of God's wrath, the exceeding sinfulness of her own heart, and of her desert of that wrath for ever, with intense sorrow for sin, and the loathsomeness of her corruptions. At times, her grief for the lost was such as to take away her bodily strength. It may be added, she survived her husband nine years, dying in the forty-ninth year of her age 1758, and to the end continuing in the love of God—

> Walking in holiness below
> To holiness above.

(4.) Now examples like this one, though they are rare, might be found in the various sections of the church of Christ, more or less remarkable. The hundred-fold is a great leap beyond the sixty and thirty-fold. And shall we not aspire to such height of attainment, that we may even here glorify the riches of the fullness of Christ, who has said that this is the privilege of believers: 'He that believeth on me, out of his inmost soul [for this is the meaning of κοιλια, the same as in Psalm 40:8, 'bowels'], shall flow *rivers of living water.*' In Exodus 24, we find all Israel alike freed from the clouds and darkness and thunderings of Sinai by the sprinkled blood of sacrifice. But notice, the mass of the people, safe indeed and happy under the clear sapphire sky, remain down at the foot of the mountain, far off comparatively; then seventy of the blood-sprinkled people ascend the height, and the power of the blood (though only *typical* blood) warrants them to go up and feast under the eye of the Holy One, the God of Israel; while one blood-sprinkled man goes up further still, even to the very seat of God, amid the glory on the mountain top. In which of these ranks would we have sought a place, had we been there that day? With the people? With the seventy elders? With Moses?

But is God's way of holiness hard to be understood? Does the hindrance to our advancement lie there? No; the Holy Ghost, the Sanctifier, has a very simple way of carrying on his work in us, if only we did not resist. He takes Christ's way; and Christ said to his disciples such things as these, *'Abide in me, and I in you'* (*John* 15:4); *'Continue ye in my love'* (*John* 15:9): that is, consciously, by faith on your part, realizing my love to you and my presence with you, go on from hour to hour in fellowship with me. The Holy Ghost 'purifies our hearts *by faith*' (*Acts* 15:9), fixing our eye on the Lord Jesus, his Cross, his Crown, himself and all his work, in sanctifying us. But we are slow to yield to the Spirit; we are not as clay to the seal.

Still this, and only this, is the way the Holy Spirit uses. In all ages it has been the same. 'We all, *with unveiled face* [It is here we so often fail: we let a veil come between us and the Lord], beholding as in a glass the glory of the Lord, are changed into the same image from glory to glory, even as by the Spirit of the Lord' (*2 Cor.* 3:18). And this is substantially the import of 1 John 5:4, 5. 'This is the victory that overcometh the world, our faith. Who is he that overcometh the world, but he who believeth that Jesus is the Son of God.' Our eye must be fixed on this mighty One, the Son of God. When in the act of beholding him we are like Stephen (*Acts* 7:55, 56), more than conquerors through him that loved us. And this is the true way in which to realize Christ 'made unto us *sanctification*' (*1 Cor.* 1:30). It is not Christ's holiness imputed to us that is meant here; but the Apostle speaks of Christ, 'our life', *imparting* holiness to us; for the order is *righteousness* by imputation, then *holiness* by impartation. Believer, have you not found it to be thus with you an hundred times? in looking unto and upon Jesus, your soul has at once felt a complete calm? You wanted patience; you betook yourself to the fullness of Christ; and as you 'considered him who endured the contradiction of sinners against himself' (*Heb.* 12:3), you became patient. Perhaps you were weak; you went to Jesus, and as you were in the act of beholding his strength, and listening to the voice that said, 'Be strong in the grace that *is in Christ Jesus*' (2 *Tim.* 2:1), you found strength imparted to you. With your eye upon him, you left it to him to fight the battle, to still the waves, to bring down the heat of temptation, to calm your temper, to bear your burden of care.

This is the divine way of rising up to our 'high places'. The Word of God nowhere says that we may in a moment reach the heights. We may have to climb upward step by step. And it would be well with many of us, to an incalculable degree, if our souls were only *constantly* from hour to hour, taking in a little of the Word that is (so to speak) the vehicle of his grace—quietly and continuously feeding on some crumb of the bread of life. Plants that grow well are taking in moisture, and drawing carbon from the atmosphere constantly, though the quantity be small. And does he not say of the vine, 'I will water it *every moment*'? (*Isa.* 27:3). If, then, it be so on his part, why not a response on ours to such amazing grace? At the same time, it will be none the less needful and desirable that we should have our frequent seasons of closer and more pro-longed communion with the Lord, for these seasons have ever left behind most blissful and transforming effects. From such seasons of prayer, meditation, direct and continued communion, you come away as from a Transfiguration; with the glory still lingering on your soul. The world would know that you had been with Jesus. In the days when the Mosque of Omar was first built, over that spot of Moriah where the worshipper could touch a piece of the unhewn original rock of the hill, it was customary to bring loads of incense and all aromatic shrubs into the shrine, which was called

Sakhrah. As a consequence, if anyone from the city had been worshipping there, he carried away with him so much of the fragrance
of the place, that when people passed him in the market-place of
Jerusalem, or in the streets, they used to say to each other, 'He has
been in the Sakhrah today!' Would to God we thus lived coming
forth daily with our 'garments smelling of the myrrh, and aloes,
and cassia, from the ivory palaces.' With fresh holiness every day
drawn out of Christ, what witnesses for him should we be! How
joyfully should we listen to the loving voice that is ever calling, 'Be
holy, for I am holy'; and he who speaks thus would hasten to give
us more and more when we repair to him.

We are 'looking for and hasting unto the coming of the day of
God' (*2 Pet.* 3:12). Now, is it not written, 'When we shall see him,
we shall be like him; for we shall see him as he is. And every man
that hath this hope in him purifieth himself, even as he is pure'?
(*1 John* 3:2-3). That Day approaches. Therefore, beloved, seeing that
we look for such things, and seeing that all present things shall so
soon be dissolved, 'what manner of persons ought we to be in all
holy conversation and godliness'?

> Had I a throne above the rest,
> Where angels and archangels dwell,
> One sin unslain within my breast
> Would make that heaven as dark as hell.
>
> The prisoner sent to breathe fresh air,
> And blest with liberty again,
> Would mourn were he condemned to wear
> One link of all his former chain.
>
> But oh! no foe invades the bliss,
> When glory crowns the Christian's head;
> One view of Jesus as He is
> Shall strike all sin for ever dead.
>
> William COWPER.

9

VICTORY OVER SIN

There is a plant called samphire, which grows only on cliffs near the sea. But though it grows near the salt waves, yet it is never found on any part of a cliff which is not above the reach of the tide. On one occasion, a party of ship-wrecked sailors flung ashore were struggling up the face of precipitous rocks, afraid of the advancing tide overtaking them, when one of their number lighted upon a plant of samphire, growing luxuriantly. Instantly he raised a shout of joy, assuring his companions by this token that they were now in safety. The sea might come near this spot, and perhaps cast up its spray, but would never be found reaching it. Such is the position of a soul in Christ; justified and united to him, the person may be in full sight still of the world's threatening and angry waves; but he is perfectly safe, and cannot be overwhelmed. Paul says of all Christians: *'Ye are risen with Christ'* (*Col.* 3:1). We are not only at peace with God; but besides, 'He hath raised us up together with Christ, and *made us sit together in heavenly places in Christ Jesus'* (*Eph.* 2:6).

Anyone who understands union to Christ will see at once what a blessed scheme it is, planned by the God of holiness, for giving a sinner victory over sin. If Lazarus be raised out of his tomb, he shall certainly be found no longer lying amid worms and rottenness, and the cold damps of the sepulchre, but walking in Bethany, in converse with living men. And so says Paul in Colossians 3:1-5:

'If ye then be risen with Christ, seek those things which are above, where Christ sitteth at the right hand of God. Set your affection on things above, not on things on the earth. For ye are dead, and your life is hid with Christ in God. When Christ, who is your life, shall appear, then shall ye also appear with him in glory. MORTIFY THEREFORE YOUR MEMBERS WHICH ARE UPON THE EARTH; *fornication, uncleanness, inordinate affection, evil concupiscence, and covetousness, which is idolatry.'* What resolutions cannot do, what vows and prayers have failed to accomplish, what self-denial and mortification and crosses have never succeeded in giving you, this plan of God at once attains,—this *union to Christ.* The sinner is led by the Holy Spirit to know and believe in the Lord Jesus, and, in the very moment of believing on him, becomes one with him. Forthwith begins a heavenly partnership: Christ and the soul share together; Christ giving to the soul out of his fullness all manner of grace, as occasion requires.

But, fellow-sinner, you must not suppose that the mere assenting to this truth as a doctrine will give you the results. You must have real experience in regard to believing in Jesus and what follows thereon. Come and try the personal application of it to your soul. Lean on Christ *for yourself,* and thus be you *yourself united* to him. Doctrine must be turned into experience. Have you read of the process by which iron is turned into steel? You will see a great crucible, with its enormous mass of iron, subjected to intense heat, till it seems a mass of glowing fire. But all that might cool down, and would be only iron after all, if there were not poured into it a small quantity of a liquid which alters every particle of its chemical constitution, and then it becomes steel. Has such a change taken place in your case: the turning the iron into steel—doctrine into experience?

We speak much of Christianity and Christians; but *union to Christ* by faith is the root of all; and faith is as much Christ's hold of us, as our hold of him. It implies our hold of the truth; but it also implies that the Spirit of truth from Christ has taken hold of us. Baptism speaks, in a figure, of souls being saved in this way of union to the Lord: for the baptized one is represented as 'baptized into him'. The Lord's Supper proclaims in another form this great truth of union to the Lord. And thus we are brought to ask all who profess to be Christ's such questions as the following:

1.—*To what does union to Christ call you?*—It calls you *to make heavenly things your business.* 'If ye be risen with Christ, seek the things which are above, where Christ sitteth at the right hand of God' (*Col.* 3:1). *Seek* such things, pursue after them, make a business of them. The word is one that implies the soul's fixed aim and employment, even as Matthew 6:33, 'Seek the kingdom of God.' 'The moment Christ rose', says Bengel, 'he was thinking of going upward' (*John* 20:17); and so it should be with us who have risen with him. The risen believer now carries on traffic with him, seeking spiritual gains. He trades for an absent Lord as eagerly as he once traded for worldly gain. He is grieved at spiritual losses as deeply as he once was at losses in his business, when a ship had foundered at sea, or a bank failed, or some speculation proved ruinous. On the other hand, he rejoices in spiritual gains: when, for example, the mist is cleared away from a truth, or when the excellency of some Scripture doctrine shines into his soul, or when he gets some fresh view of Christ, and some increase of faith, love, and hope. More specially still, he fixes his attention habitually upon *Christ sitting at the right hand;* for his being there tells so much about acceptance. His 'sitting' declares that he has finished all his undertaking, and has no more toil to undergo. His 'sitting at the right hand' declares the Father's high approval, and delight, and honour. And so to this point he ever turns his eye,—to this mountain of myrrh. And in truth he finds yet more there: he finds that by virtue of union to Christ he is himself, in a sense, there also, 'sitting in heavenly places', his toil done, his trials over, his victory won, himself altogether well-pleasing to the Father, and loved by the Father. The realization of this privilege has mighty power upon his soul; giving him wondrous liberty, helping his near communion, sending him forth to ever new and grateful service for One who so loves him.

It calls on you *to disentangle your affection from earth*. 'Set your affection on things above, not on things on the earth' (*Col.* 3:2). Make the things above your care; they are to be 'the things which you mind', in opposition to such men as those spoken of (*Phil.* 3:19), who mind earthly things. You will not be content with making those things your business; you will have a taste and relish for them, a real delight in them. Many men pursue business with little liking for the thing itself, and are glad when it is over. Many an industrious and eager trader longs for rest and retirement. But the believer risen with Christ loves his business, his whole heart is in it. He minds—cares for, has affection for—'not things on earth', such as to be rich, great, noble, enjoy pleasure, nor even domestic comfort and personal ease. His chief end is not earthly prosperity, nor is his highest bliss the possession of a few more acres than other men; but it is *'things above'* which he relishes so heartily and unfeignedly. He is at home among 'things above'. He is like the patriarchs, who left all they had in their native land, seeking 'a better, that is, a heavenly country'. Such men mind God's favour, God's glory, God's love. And hence, their children's salvation is more to them than their aggrandisement in the world; and the conversion of souls than the news of mines of gold discovered and secured.

Do you bear the name of *Christian?* Is this, then, a fair account of you? Speak not of difficulties; for of course there are such in all pursuits; and here all alleged hindrances are swept out of the way by that word: *'If ye be risen with Christ'*. This word cuts the string, and the balloon ascends.

2.—*What does union to Christ ensure to you?*—It ensures many

things; but here are some. It ensures *your getting life from Christ.*
'For ye are dead, and your life is hid with Christ in God' (*Col.* 3:3).
You who are Christ's *died with him*, and in that hour your former
life passed away. You had lived it out; it was for ever over, and
you were loosed from all former things. *You died.* It was as if you
had been carried to the New Earth at once, to live evermore there
amidst its holy scenes; as if to you that day had come in which
Christ says, 'Behold I make all things new.' You became a 'new
creature', part of a new creation, one with Christ, so that you lost
your former separateness. And you found that, while you had lost
your old life, there was new life laid up for you. *'Life was hid for you
with Christ in God.'* You got the beginnings of a far better life than
even unfallen Adam had, for you got life from Christ. Christ's very
life is yours; the very sap of the vine-tree for you the branch; the
same resurrection life which the Spirit poured into the man Christ
Jesus was now yours also.

That holy power to love God and man, which was in Christ,
you began to receive. That holy joy and intensely real delight in
God's favour, which on earth was Christ's endowment, and ever
is, became your portion. And you go on claiming every day a share
in his stores of grace, a share in his holiness, a share in the Spirit's
manifold blessings. Light, life, likeness, all are yours, by gift.

The moment you believed, you were united to Christ; and that
moment the stone was rolled off the mouth of the well; you began
to get the new life, and you had it more or less ever since. But you
have as yet only the beginnings of it. As when a father leaves for his
son, while yet a minor, a portion, but only a portion, of the property, which is given out by some trustee; so you at present receive
only in measure. *'The life'*, in all its fullness, *'is hid with Christ'*; that
is, Christ has it, and Christ who has it is 'hid', or concealed like laid
up treasure, but *'hid in God'*, in the bosom of the Father, so that all
is safe and sure. It is hid, like the manna in the golden pot, within

the holy of holies. It is there for safety, 'as men lay up jewels in a place where the short arms of children cannot reach them', says Samuel Rutherford; 'for if it was in our keeping, it would soon be lost.' But all is *kept for us,* as 1 Peter 1:4 declares. It is 'our life' (*Col.* 3:4), life which we have a claim to, stored up for us, intended for us. Yes, *Christ* is 'our life'; Christ is, so to speak, keeping himself for us, and keeping for us the life abundantly which he purchased for us.

But again, this union to Christ ensures *your appearing with Christ in glory.* 'When Christ, who is our life, shall appear, then shall we also appear with him in glory' (*Col.* 3:4). At present the believer, though one with Christ, lives outwardly as other men do: eating, drinking, sleeping, trading: he sows, he sails, he travels on railways, he goes to buy and sell, he reads news, he talks with his friends and children,—all as other men. But all the while he has an interior life; he has a strong taste for spiritual things; he has desires toward God which other men know not of; he yearns after God in Christ amid earth's fairest scenes; he loves God in Christ beyond wife, or children, or parents, or possessions. 'None of us liveth to himself' (*Rom.* 14:7). And this life is preparing to bud forth into flower and fruit, whenever the present winter of earth has passed, and the Sun of righteousness arisen.

On the day when God's time arrives for giving the larger full-ness of the life to all who are members of Christ's body—on that day, 'Christ our life shall appear.'The golden pot of manna, hidden long, shall be brought out of the Holy Place. He shall be fully in us, and we fully in him. He shall appear who is 'our life'—he on whom we nourish our souls—who has life for us—who is himself the substance of that life, for (as one said) 'Christ is a Christian's life.' He shall appear, bringing this life to us; and this life which he brings shall, at the same time, be the secret cause of 'glory' to us; or, perhaps we should rather say, this life shall manifest its pres-ence in us by our being forthwith invested with glory. As when a fountain gushes over, its waters make all round the margin green and flourishing; so, when our life gushes into us our very bodies shall beam with glory. It was thus on the Transfiguration-hill with Christ himself. The life in him that evening—the secret well of life—suddenly overflowed, rising up to the brim; and see! what a body! yea, what garments even! And who could tell the joy of his soul in that hour, though he knew that sorrow was to return again to its channel, and fill up all its banks! Now thus it shall be with us,—ay, thus it shall be with us without any after return to sorrow, without any risk of the waters abating. Some weary day draws to its evening; we have wiped the sweat from our brow, and sighed over earth; we have groaned within ourselves, 'Oh, who shall deliver me from the body of this death!' when lo! the sudden flash! It is the coming of the Son of man.

You may at times have envied Moses and Elijah their blessed position, on either side of Jesus, *'appearing in glory'* (*Luke* 9:31). But you yourself shall be as they: *'Then shall ye also appear with him in glory.'* Yes, as truly *'with him'* as they were; as bright as they *'in glory';* seeing Christ, talking with Christ, hearing the voice that proclaims, *'This is my beloved Son!'* O Master, O King of glory, O our Life, appear! Come forth from that light inaccessible, to be ever with us! No need of three tabernacles: for thy tabernacle shall be there, and all shall ever say, as the ages roll, 'It is good to be here.' That will be the day which accomplishes what many in the church of God have often sung:

> One look of Jesus as He is,
> Shall strike all sin for ever dead.

3. *What does union to Christ ensure to you even now?*—It enables us to overcome the world, and to renounce all sin; for the Spirit dwells in every believer. 'MORTIFY THEREFORE your members which are upon the earth' (*Col.* 3:5). We do not yet and now over-

come self, and the world, and Satan, in the manner we shall do when Christ appears, when (as old Sibbes triumphantly exclaims) 'we shall trample down foes in glorious confusion!' But we, nevertheless, do overcome; for that strain is a true one:

> Neither passion nor pride Thy cross can abide,
> But melt in the fountain that flows from Thy side.

'MORTIFY therefore',—that is, make dead, reduce to a state of death as regards your practice of them, and care for them,—'*members which are on the earth*'; your hands, eyes, feet, are not to meddle with '*fornication, uncleanness, inordinate affection, evil concupiscence, and covetousness.*' Whatever is yours belongs now to Christ, and is instinct with Christ's Spirit; not merely *ought to be*, but really *is* so. Therefore, as men who are possessed of the power so to do—as men who have the life within you, ready to be used—control your members though they be still on the earth and in the presence of its objects. The fire is around you; but you have the supply of water beside you: make it play upon these flames, that they may not even singe a hair of your head. With your eye on things above, with your heart realizing your union to Christ, trample down the world and sin. In the power of your union to Christ, reckoning yourselves as one with him, go forth and conquer. It is he that conquers. You go forth appealing to him: 'Lord, I am one with thee: canst thou be overcome?' In so doing, believers find lust sinks away, and passions grow cool, and covetousness relaxes its grasp; all tempting sin gives up its struggle for victory.

We might bring forward thousands of witnesses. Let us give the experience of one as a sample,—the experience of one man who had yielded himself to sin and lust freely, and for long years. This man was led to listen to the gospel plan, under the preaching of Joseph Milner, the writer of the *Church History*. The text explained was 2 Corinthians 5:20, 21—reconciliation to God over him who 'was made sin for us, that we might be made the righteousness of God in him.' John Howard heard it—was overcome; all the happiness he ever enjoyed before was felt by him to be no more like it than midnight darkness to the noonday sun. From that moment all his strong passions died away. The man who used to be shunned by all who cared for chastity and purity, felt himself suddenly delivered from the power of his lusts, so remarkably indeed that from that hour, he was no more overcome; nay, from that hour all was soberness and calmness of spirit. He used to say, that his enjoyment of God dried up the streams of sinful concupiscence, as it did long ago in the case of Augustine. And this is God's way of holiness. Legalists, and moralists, and philosophers, all fail in reaching the seat of the evil—the will and the desire; they lop the branches, but do not reach the root; they imprison the felon, but do not change his nature. To overcome evil within, St Benedict rolled himself on thorns; St Martin burnt his flesh with hot irons; St Francis tumbled in snow; St Bernard plunged himself in pools of freezing water. Even the great Pascal wore an iron girdle, full of sharp points, next his skin. All these overlooked, or understood not, the apostle's inspired words, 'Mortify THEREFORE'; that is, conscious of your union to Christ, set about the mortifying of your members in the strength of this union, and in no other way. Think of union to Christ, and how it involves partnership with him in his grace. Believing thus in him is our victory: doing, resolving, suffering, give us no victory at all. The fear of hell and wrath will scarcely keep a man from one sin, and will never touch the heart.

Who of you then have, in time past, failed to triumph over your corruptions, and evil propensities? Who of you has never been able to master covetousness? or the world in any shape? Take the way of believing in Christ, and being thus in partnership with him, understand the blessed mystery of 'rising with Christ', and being seated with him above; be grafted into the vine, and get its sap. You have tried other means of health and strength; but now use this inspired direction, which has never failed. As Daniel and his fellows asked to be proved whether the water and the pulse they were nourished on would not turn out far more strengthening than all the king's finest food and rarest wines, so we say to you, Prove it now for yourselves. And do not say, 'I will wait for the Spirit'; for by that you mean, 'I will wait on till I *feel* the Spirit at work.' This is a device of Satan to get you to go on in sin, and die in sin; for no man ever felt the Spirit at work directly. The Spirit works in silence. The soul learns the gospel way, and ponders it; muses on Christ, who died and rose, and who calls on sinners every one, to come and use his death and resurrection. And it is while the sinner is thus engaged before the cross, that the Holy Spirit works effectually—uniting him to Christ in the same moment that he leads him to Christ. And so the believing man becomes at once a conqueror!

WINNING CHRIST

For a man to have 'won Christ', in the scriptural sense of the term, would be the same thing as 'having already attained', and 'being already perfect'. So great is this subject, 'Winning Christ'. Why, then, attempt to handle so great a subject? We seek to be enabled, by the grace and Spirit of God, to point out what a wondrous pursuit it is, that all may engage in it for themselves. The Alpine guide can take the traveller to a point from which he will see the scenery of the prospect that is so immense; but he does not undertake to look for the traveller. If I had been a shepherd lad at Bethlehem in the day when Christ was born, I could have done what the star did for the wise men. I could have said, 'There is the spot where the babe, the new-born King of the Jews, is lying', and then have left it to themselves to go in and gaze, and drink in the mystery of godliness which was before them. That is all we do in speaking of 'winning Christ'.

1. *'Winning Christ'* is not *finding Christ*, nor is it being *found in Christ*. These are the two extremes. The one is the starting point, and the other—being 'found in him'—is the goal. But between these two lies the *'winning Christ'*. Paul, who uses that expression in Philippians 3:8, at the time he so wrote, had been about thirty years in Christ. Thirty years before, he had found Christ, and Christ had found him, on the road to Damascus. He had been the ringleader of self-righteousness, a man who, of all sinners in

the world, was the most determined enemy of Jesus, the righteous One. How he was arrested on the road to Damascus, how for three days he lay in darkness, feeling what he was as a sinner, is known to all. Anyone passing up the street called Straight, might hear from that house groanings as of a deadly wounded man. It is Saul of Tarsus; into whose soul God's arrows have sunk. But at the end of the three days it pleased God to reveal his Son in him. He got such a discovery of Christ that, from that hour, he never took his eye off from him, but lived his life 'looking unto Jesus'. He saw in him what made him lose all conceit of whatever he had known of earthly glory. Has there been such a time in your life? Can every one who reads these lines say, 'There has been in my lifetime a period when I was made to know that hitherto I had been blind, and then was made to see the Lord Jesus all my righteousness, all my strength'?

After that day it was Paul's constant aim to go on in Christ; that he might be found in him when the Lord should call him, or come for him. We have said that he went on in this pursuit of Christ, never taking his eye off him. If you had met him the third day after that wonderful change, you would have found him gazing upon Christ, and discovering new glory in him. Had you met him thirty years after, when he penned the words which the Holy Ghost gave him, 'That I may win Christ', you would have seen him still gazing on the same Christ. He had not changed the object of his gaze, and he meant to continue thus till he was *found in Christ*.

Very often it happens in the experience of believers who are running this race, that they fail, after a few years, to see what Paul saw in Christ. Sometimes they begin to look aside to something they have done. Very often you find a believing man, insensibly, unconsciously, trusting in his trust. Another is getting spiritually proud, though not aware of it—he fancies he has attained to some superior grace, and is no longer satisfied with what he began with.

He is not quite content with seeing in Christ the same salvation that he saw at the first,—'Christ made sin for us that we might be made the righteousness of God in him'—Christ 'made a curse for us', that the blessing might come down on us without stint or measure. He begins to turn aside a little from this truth. Just as if the prodigal, after having been a little while at his father's table, wearing the best robe, feeding on the fatted calf, had begun to wish he had, besides what his father furnished, some by-table of his own, not caring to be wholly indebted, as at the first, to his father's bounty and love. There is a tendency of this kind in us all. In various ways it manifests itself; and hence it is that we, believers, need to be 'winning Christ' every day, and every hour of the day, if we would escape this tendency. It was because Paul was always 'winning Christ' that he never deviated from the straight path.

2. The word 'winning' is the same as *gaining*. 'If a man should *gain* the whole world.' It is the word used in Matthew 16:26. It is also used for merchants gaining by their trade; so that the meaning of *winning* Christ is, gaining out of Christ the riches that are in him, the wealth that is stored up in him. It is an interesting fact, that in Wales and in Scotland, in the mining districts, 'winning' the coal, or the mineral, is a common expression, by which they mean, sinking a shaft deep down to get out the ore in richer abundance.—Let us take that idea. Paul, on the day when he first discovered Christ, found himself to be the possessor of a large estate. He was standing, so to speak, at the opening of this mine, and he saw some of the precious ore. He could not take his eye off what he did see; but, the more he looked, the more he discovered of the inexhaustible riches there. He had only to dig down, to sink his shaft in all directions, and there was no end to what he might bring up out of this mine; and so it was his lifetime's wish, 'that I may win Christ'. When he had got some of this ore, he was inflamed with a desire to get more. He would stand amid the heaps of his gold and say,

'That I may win Christ!' This is my heart's desire, my life's end and aim.' Is it yours? Have you discovered that there are riches in Christ such as those we speak of?

An eminent preacher in other days, Dr Conyers, began his ministry out of Christ. Christ was unknown to him, except by name. But on one occasion, in the lesson of the day, he read the words, 'The unsearchable riches of Christ.' Unsearchable riches! These two words caught his attention during the service; and, when he went home, he opened his Greek Bible, that he might see if those actually were the terms—if those English terms really expressed the original. He saw they did; that the word 'unsearchable' was a word that meant, 'that could not be searched out'. The thought arose in his heart, 'Then I have been in ignorance of Christ all my lifetime.' God made that the beginning of his inquiry after Christ; and not long after he was found pacing his room, clapping his hands for joy, and exclaiming, 'I have found him! I have found him! "The blood of Jesus Christ his Son cleanseth us from all sin!"' There you see a man winning Christ—getting at the unsearchable riches.

We have seen how Paul was eager in this matter. But let us look at it again. It is not only to win *something* out of him. Paul was so highly ambitious that he says, 'I want to *win Christ, all* Christ. I would fain have him all, with all his riches.' And did it ever occur to you as strange that Paul should not say, 'that I may win *souls*'? Many, I dare say, would have liked if Paul had said more expressly that he lived to win souls. But Paul prefers to say, 'that I may win *Christ*'. If a man wins Christ, and gets at his unsearchable riches, there is no question but he will discover much about himself and sin. The prophet Isaiah, when he saw the King, the Lord of Hosts, on the throne, in a moment felt self was withered into nothingness. And just as little doubt is there that a man who wins much of Christ's riches will win souls. Who has not observed, that when those who conduct meetings, and have been at the first greatly blessed, afterwards lose their power, it is almost without exception, because they have not been *winning Christ?* They have been giving out what they once had, just the same thing over and over again, but making no advance, getting no fresh insight into Christ; and so their words have begun to fall without power. The audience, though they cannot define what the difference is, soon know that there is a difference. There never can be the same unction and power when a man is not winning Christ, bringing out fresh ore from the mine, and laying it down before the hearer. If, therefore, we would he more useful, there is no other way but this of our text. This is the shorthand method. Win Christ every day, and the Holy Ghost will bless what you tell of him, for he delights to glorify Christ.

3. *But how are we to carry on this winning?* How are we to proceed in every day seeking to win Christ? Let us invariably begin with the *Person* of Christ. Let us seek to be taught that most wondrous mystery—God-man. If ever we begin to think that we have seen all that we need to see in the Person of Christ, we have made a very great mistake—a mistake that will affect all our after-growth. No; through eternity we shall be exploring the person of Christ. For in that person everything that is wondrous meets. There you have the Creator and the creature in one, the finite and the infinite, the visible and the invisible. There you have humanity married to Divinity. A most wondrous mystery, the person of Christ, God-man! Let us always take Christ's person with us, whatever subject in connection with him we are about to explore.

And with this before us, see what follows. I want to look at Christ's *obedience* for me—that obedience by which I am made righteous; for, 'by the obedience of One shall many be made righteous' (*Rom.* 5:19). Here is Christ obeying the law—God-man obeying it, God-man casting around that law all the lustre that the obedience of such a person can cast around it; magnifying it, and making it honourable. And when this obedience is placed to my account, and I am accounted righteous in the Righteous One, I have wealth of obedience to present to God. I have the obedience of the God-man. Nothing, then, of my disobedience can in any way stand before me and my title to the full reward.

Then we look at his *suffering*—his suffering all his life long—and the completing of it in his death, when he drank the dregs of the cup, and left nothing remaining. The most awful agony, the most unspeakably great suffering that words can even hint at—all these agonies had a meaning in them that no other possibly can have. Every groan and every tear of the *God-man* had deep significance. There was an aged minister in Scotland, in the days of my boyhood, who on one occasion made an audience sink into perfect silence by a very simple remark. Having read out the words, 'Jesus wept', he looked round and said: 'Ye know what weeping means.' He then looked at them again, and said, 'Ye know who Jesus was.' *'Jesus wept!'* One tear of the God-man, what meaning it had! What power to atone! Put all that he presented to the Father, put it before you, and you have infinite satisfaction given to the law's penalty. And now you see the meaning of his being 'made sin for us, that we might be made the righteousness of God in him' (*2 Cor.* 5:21)—'made a curse for us, that the blessing might come upon us' (*Gal.* 3:13, 14). What righteousness! what blessing! since he was the Person through whom it came to us. Are there not unsearchable riches here! No mistake can be greater than to think we have exhausted the meaning of these things, that we learned at the first. They are to be our life-study.

And so when we call to mind our *union* to him. We are his members. To be a complete Christ he cannot want one of his members, so thoroughly are we one with him. My Mediator—think who he is. All in him is given to me. Then no wonder that I have *joy*. The wonder is that I am not overflowing with a joy that is full of glory.

No wonder I have *peace;* the only wonder is that I have anything else than 'peace that passes all understanding'. All the sunshine that falls upon the vine falls upon the branches, and if I am a branch I have the Father's sunshine of love. And the sap of that vine belongs to me. All that is in Christ belongs to me. Believer, should we not wonder daily that we take so little from him, that we win so few victories through him! Instead of wondering that we are said to be 'more than conquerors' (*Rom.* 8:37), we should rather say it must always be so, because we are one with him.

One thing further. When carrying on our researches and exploring the mine, let us never forget to look at him as he shall be revealed. We are to win Christ as he is to be revealed. Look at him in his coming glory. We gladly take what his Cross has purchased. We gladly take all that his Resurrection and Ascension bring us. We gladly look up to an Interceding Saviour. But look to a *Coming Saviour,* at his coming in glory as the Bridegroom—as the King of kings and the Lord of lords. What does he say to you in prospect of that day? He says, 'I am the bright and morning Star'; and does he not at the same time say to us *'I will give you the morning Star'* (*Rev.* 2:28), I will give you myself in my glory? All the glory in which I am to be manifested on that day belongs to you. What a prospect this opens up to us! For is he not called 'our life' when he appears!—'Christ our life shall appear and we shall appear with him in glory' (*Col.* 3:4). The fullness of life and of glory seem to go together. Should we not then be seeking to win more in this direction?

There is no limit to the treasure we may thus win out of Christ. I was once visiting a family, who, I knew, had formerly been in a part of the country where there were mines. I said, 'How is it that you have come away from what was so long your residence?' The answer was, 'The mineral was all exhausted',—and so they had betaken themselves to another spot, for there was nothing more to be got in that mine. Shall this ever be the case with Christ? Yet does it not seem as if some believers thought that, at any rate in some directions, they had got all that can be got? How strange the mistake to think that inexhaustible riches have been exhausted! As yet you have only begun to know a very little of Christ.

And here it is important to speak of 'searching the Scriptures'. It is in them you have eternal life set forth—they are they which testify of Jesus (*John* 5:39).

(a) If you are *conscious of still being unconverted,* search the Scriptures in order to find the hid treasure. This is Christ's own suggestion, for listen to his parable (*Matt.* 13:44). Yonder is a man, busy and diligent, head and hands full of work. He thinks of no riches but what his own ploughing, and digging, and sowing may bring. One day, however, he espies beneath the surface something glittering—it is silver! it is gold! Here is a new way of reaching his goal! '*This is a new kind of new treasure,* and let me make it my own!' A thought about Christ has been shot into his soul—thoughts of another world, and of him who is all our salvation, and all our desire, have got entrance. He sees where true wealth lies, and how he may become rich now, by simply taking what Christ won for him.

(b) And if you *are a believer,* search the Scriptures in order to find more treasure. It is in the Word he meets us; it is by the Word he reveals to us his riches. We must daily repair to the field where the treasure lies, and explore what is to be found there—what the Scriptures set forth in Old Testament and New, by word and by sign, by teaching and by parable, by type and anti-type, by prophecy and fulfilment, by history and by song, and by epistles. Never forget that Joshua (see chap. 1:8) was told that his prosperity in all his undertakings would depend on his 'meditating on the Law of God day and night'; and that that counsel was embodied in the first of the Songs of Israel (*Psa.* 1:2, 3). *Study the Bible;* the sixty-six holy books given us by the Holy Ghost. Study every page and line of *God's letter* to the sons of men. Who can tell what you will win daily?

4. It is quite evident that the soul that is every day carrying on this winning will not be a backsliding soul. Assuredly, if the Holy Spirit enable you day by day to carry on this pursuit, you will be kept from backsliding. Every fresh discovery of Christ is a security against turning aside. We begin to backslide whenever we let dimness in looking to Christ come over our eye. No sooner do we let him out of sight, than we begin to draw back. If you would be vigorous in your spiritual life, win Christ; if you would be useful, win Christ; if you would be happy, win him every day. If you would grow, win Christ. It is somewhat like astronomy. Every discovery that is made helps us on to greater discoveries. You never hear the astronomer saying, 'We may stop now in our exploration of the heavens', when a great discovery is made. On the contrary, it impels him to go on more vigorously than ever. Let it be so with God's children.

Shall we not be continually letting unsaved men know that we have got what they might well envy? Surely if they saw us winning Christ, and finding what delighted us, and kept us ever searching further, they might be allured. If they saw that we had got a rich secret they knew nothing of, it would draw some, who fancy, when they hear only a few common-place words about Christ, often repeated, that there is very little in Christ. Unsaved souls, come and inquire into this matter. Begin where Paul began, at the foot of the Cross. Begin by recognizing Christ as your Saviour from guilt and wrath, by seeing Christ made sin, made curse for us, that we might be made the righteousness of God in him (*2 Cor.* 5:21). Come and see this, and see it now. You have no time to lose. The missionary Judson once spoke to a Burmese prince who seemed in earnest about salvation, and pressed him at once to admit the claims of Christ, the Son of God. The thoughtful prince said he would consider. It was worth considering, Judson said, 'But make up your mind: it is too important a matter only to consider.' The prince said, 'It is too great a matter to decide on all at once.' Judson asked, 'When do you mean to make up your mind?' He said something to the effect that he would speak about it again next week. Judson looked at him and replied, 'What if, in the meantime, you change worlds?' Fellow-sinner, unsaved soul, you may have changed worlds before tomorrow; make up your mind now to accept this Saviour, this Christ, and to spend time and eternity in 'winning him'.

THE CONVERSION OF CHILDREN

There is a practical error very common among God's people. All of them profess to believe that the Holy Spirit may convert souls at any age, and that conversion cannot take place too soon; while yet they do not look for the conversion of children with the same lively faith that they manifest in asking and expecting the Holy Spirit to change those who are of riper years. The same warm-hearted believers who labour for the souls of older persons, and are, in the case of such, satisfied with nothing but conversion without delay, do not practically so feel and act in dealing with the young. They are satisfied if the young give attention to the truth, and if they seem not unwilling to retain in their thoughts what they learn. They do not press home *the immediate, present, acceptance of Christ on children* as they would do on grown-up persons. They would go home from any other meeting disappointed, sad, and unsatisfied, if, night after night, souls were unawakened and unsaved, though attentive and interested; and yet, in the case of children, they can allow of delay—they can leave their Sabbath class or their family circle without alarm and without anxiety, though there be therein no symptom of real awakening, and no evidence of these young souls finding the Saviour.

One reason for the difference thus made in the case of the young is, with many, the misunderstanding of certain texts of Scripture— at least so we are strongly inclined to think. Thus,

1. One person quotes Proverbs 22:6, 'Train up a child in the way he should go, and when he is old he will not depart from it.' The person with whom this text is a favourite probably applies it thus—'Only teach the plan of salvation to a child, and show wisdom's happy ways to a child, and, though at the time the child be not converted, yet, when he is old, he will no doubt take the way you have taught him.' But is this true? and is this the sense of the text? Very far from it. The Holy Spirit means to teach us quite another lesson by these words, viz., 'Only be sure that you get the child in the way *while still a child,* and you need never fear in regard to that child's after perseverance.' It is, 'Initiate a child in the way' (see the Hebrew), or at the beginning of the way: get the truth introduced into his soul while he is a child, and rest assured that he shall go on as he has begun. It is a blessed text to encourage us to seek the *present and immediate conversion* of children.

2. Another person uses a figure, and soothes his conscience under lack of success, in his class or in his family, by saying, 'Well, at any rate I am filling the water-pots with water (*John* 2:7), so that there shall be the greater amount of wine at a future day, when at length the water is turned into wine by the Lord's miraculous power, in the hour of conversion.' Now this is only a figurative application of a text, and no argument at all. But, even using their own figure, how is it that they do not expect the turning of the water into wine to be immediate? What is there in the passage to which they allude to warrant their waiting on till a distant time? Was not the water changed into wine in these water-pots in a single hour? Indeed, it seems that the change took place in the very act of filling the vessels.

3. A third person has much to say, in a doctrinal form, on the text in Philippians 1:6, 'He that has begun the good work will perform it', applying the passage to feelings, impressions, interest awakened among the young in the course of common, weekly teaching.

There is no conversion in such cases: but then it is alleged, 'There is real interest felt, there is impression made, and so the good work is begun and, if begun, shall go on.' We reply, there is a serious mistake here, for 'the good work begun' means that *conversion* has taken place; *conversion* is the *good work* that begins the Christian life. Read the context, and see this beyond doubt or dispute. The apostle says, 'He that has converted you, placing you on Christ the foundation, will not forsake you, but will carry on the building to completeness in the day of Christ's appearing.' So that this text is really an argument in favour of our not being content with anything in the form of mere impression, hopeful interest, conviction. We must see conversion-work, we must see salvation-work, we must see the Christian life really begun. And this applies to the case alike of old and young.

There is, farther, apart from and besides all this, a secret feeling on the part of many Christians that it is not so important, nor so great a service, to be the means of converting children as it is to be the means of converting adults. They have no scripture proof of this view; for 'converting a sinner' means any sinner, young as well as old; and 'turning many to righteousness' includes young and old; and 'winning souls' limits us to no age. But nevertheless such persons feel, without putting their feelings into words, that it is a more palpable and evident gain to win an intelligent adult than to win his child to Christ. Now, this quiet persuasion (appearing in their practice), may arise from the thought that these adults are of present value in society: their conversion will at once affect society; while the conversion of the young is at the time unfelt beyond the circle of the family and a few companions. But, on the other hand, they forget that young souls, brought to Christ in very infancy, will be exercising an influence, year by year, all life long, in all the different stages of their growth, and at length, on reaching manhood, will, by God's grace, mightily move for good their circle of society—over and above the consideration of the evils escaped and the ill that was never done.

There is, however, a more serious misapprehension lying at the root of this undervaluing of early conversion. In reality, many godly people do look upon the conversion of children as a thing *to be stood in doubt of.* They scarcely believe that any child's conversion is so deep and genuine as that of an adult. They admit that all conversion alike is the work of the Holy Ghost, and that he does, when it pleases him, convert children as well as adults. Still, they habitually ignore apparent conversion in children; they have a theory that children imitate old people, and that therefore these appearances are to be put down to imitation only. In dealing with such persons we say—

(a) There must surely be cases of real conversion among children, if the Word of God is to be our standard; for surely Psalm 8:2, is written for all ages, and our Lord has commented upon it thus, in Matthew 21:16, 'Have ye never read, Out of the mouth of babes and sucklings thou hast perfected praise'? If 'old men and *children*' alike are called on (*Psa.* 148:12) to praise the Lord, surely it is implied that they are alike capable of saving grace. Indeed, for one moment to suppose the matter otherwise would be to assert that the gospel is not suited to the souls of the young.[1]

(b) There is a peculiar fitness (we might say, divine propriety) in the gospel being blessed to the conversion of children. The same Holy Spirit in all cases uses the gospel for saving souls; but, in applying it to children, he illustrates most notably two of its features, viz., its entire freeness (for what could a child give to God?), and its amazing simplicity, which is so humbling to the pride of self-righteous man. 'I thank thee, O Father, that thou hast hid

---

[1] A little girl's reply to the question, 'When should children come to Christ?' was excellent. One scholar had answered, 'At thirteen.' Another, 'At ten.' Another, 'At six.' But her reply was, 'Whenever they understand who God is.'

these things from the wise and prudent, and hast *revealed them unto babes*' (*Luke* 10:21, and as Jesus said this, '*He rejoiced* in spirit'). 'Whosoever shall not receive the kingdom of God as a little child shall in no wise enter therein' (*Luke* 18:17). Nothing was done by the babes or little children whom Christ blessed but this, they let him lift them up in his arms without resistance, and received what he gave without offering him any price in return!

(c) The drawing love of the cross of Christ (looking for a moment at the matter from man's point of view) surely appeals as readily and suitably to the hearts of children as to adults. Nay, is it not into the young heart that we might expect such kindness and love should find entrance, even if older souls were unmoved by it?

(d) The doctrine of the substitution of Christ for sinners, 'the Just for the unjust', 'the Shepherd for the sheep', is the very heart and essence of the gospel; and is not this the very truth of all others that finds entrance into the understanding of any child? We do not now speak of the heart or conscience, but of the understanding. Even a very child can be made to apprehend the meaning of *Substitution*—of the One for the many; just as the 'Happy Mute' was made at once to see how the giving of one gold ring for thousands of withered leaves was an over-payment in exchange. Hence it is always this grand truth that we ought to press on the very youngest soul. We tell them, 'You are sinners, exposed to God's wrath and curse, and you cannot save yourselves; but God's own Son can save you, by Himself bearing that wrath and curse.' In some such form as this the Spirit brings in faith to a child's soul; and, once received, is not this truth the same in its effects on the young as on the old? Is not the text John 1:12 as true in the case of a child as in the instance of an intelligent adult, 'As many as received him, to them gave he power to become the sons of God'?

Children ought to be dealt with, in regard to the duty of accepting Christ, as closely and seriously as older people. The difference, no doubt, is considerable in the method we take with the young and with the older. In the former case, we have no metaphysical difficulties to deal with. We find, however, the same need in both cases of being like Nathan in his parable; we need to look the old man and the child alike in the face, and say, 'You are meant. Will you accept the Saviour who has saved so many by taking on him their sins, and bearing their punishment?' Personal dealing is required; a dealing with them one by one.

Many Christian people are not sufficiently aware of the importance of a *personal question;* whether the individual be old or young. I have seen an aged person struck as with an arrow on being solemnly asked, face to face, 'Have you been born again?' and exclaiming, 'Have *I* myself been born again! the question was never so put to my soul till now.' I have known a young man brought to a stand at once by the personal question, 'Do you accept Christ now?' And so also I have seen a child strongly moved by such a direct appeal, though before listening only playfully. This seems to be the Spirit's favourite way of inserting the point of the wedge that is to split the cedar. Teachers and parents, is it not worth trying this way?

In the early part of this century there were Associations for Sabbath School Teaching in Edinburgh and elsewhere, consisting of warm-hearted men who delighted to show the gospel to others. These directed their main efforts toward the conversion of children. We have heard some of those old Christians tell how they never let the classes go without drawing out the gospel from the lesson, and seeking to carry it home by apt illustrations. They were not content with sending them away to pray; they sent them to *Christ* on the spot. The result was that there were many brought to Christ at an early age in the Sabbath Schools. We have heard of even startling cases occurring, such as a case of clear evidence of conversion given by a child of four years of age.

But we ask again, why do many in our day regard with suspicion cases of very early conversion?

1. One reason seems to be, they fancy that every manifestation of delight in and love to Christ is altogether a matter of *feeling*, and not of *faith*, in these children. Now, if it were so, they would have some good grounds for their scepticism. But then we assert that the evidence goes to prove the opposite; for these young people furnish full evidence of faith in the Lord Jesus; and we complain that they who doubt it have not taken sufficient pains to inquire. They got their data at second hand. They do not go and get acquainted with the cases by personal converse.

2. Another reason alleged for their doubt is, that these children do not manifest holiness in the way in which it is manifested in adults. Well, that is true; but children's play, and children's natural buoyancy, should no more come in the way of believing their real conversion, than should, in older people, their occasional and engrossing care and anxiety about business. Children's conscientiousness in lessons, and fairness in playing games, and command of temper, may yield as true a proof of sanctification begun, as do the integrity of the adult, and his firm adherence to principle in matters of merchandise. It is quite true that in the case of a child we may more easily mistake feeling for faith than in the case of a grown-up person; but this only calls for patient attention and caution on our part; it does not discredit the reality of faith in the case of those who manifest it, and the evidences of whose faith we have opportunity of knowing.

Of late, in our country, an American minister, Rev. E. Payson Hammond, has done much to fix attention on the subject of early conversions. He holds, as fully as any man, that conversion is the work of the Holy Ghost, and he believes the sovereignty of divine grace as much as any other Calvinist; but he also believes that the Holy Ghost, in the exercise of gracious sovereignty, is pleased to work by the gospel on *very young souls,* as really as on adults. And so he sets himself to ply young souls with the gospel, and to insist on their immediate acceptance of it.

Several things in Mr Hammond's dealings with children deserve special notice. One is, his firm persuasion that the gospel is *'the power of God unto salvation' in the case of the youngest* that has understanding. He goes to his meetings never doubting; and goes to work accordingly. He tells the gospel-story, presses it home, and calls for a present acceptance of Christ on the part of the children. He does not feel content with delivering his message, saying, 'Now I have sown the seed, let us hope it may spring up some time after this.' No he looks for 'God giving the increase' at the time, just as at Pentecost.

Another feature in Mr Hammond's method is, *the form in which he preaches the gospel.* It is, in the main, that of Substitution. Not that he always, or even very often, uses that word; but that is his leading idea in setting forth the way of salvation. He perhaps starts with a text that involves that truth; then he brings in stories to illustrate his text, using illustrations which are not always perhaps quite solemn, but which always end in conveying the truth of sub-stitution to the understanding and heart—if not also, at the same time, flashing into the conscience of the youngest the *sin of refusing such a substitute as Jesus.* The sum of his address is just this—

Jesus, from His throne on high
Came into this world to die;
That I might from sin be free,
Bled and died upon the tree.

I can see Him even now,
With His pierced, thorn-clad brow,
Agonizing on the tree,
Oh, what love! and all for me.

Now I feel this heart of mine
Drawn to love God's holy Son, etc.

There never is, with Mr Hammond, the possibility of your mistaking or forgetting the grand end in view. To many a Sabbath School teacher—ay, and to many a minister—there is too much reason to fear that Mr Cecil's story of himself is only too truly applicable. Mr Cecil tells how, on one occasion, when labouring under trouble that caused him great suffering, and which baffled all ordinary physicians, he was guided to an illustrious physician, who at once told him, 'There is only one remedy; do try it—it is perfectly simple', mentioning the medicine. Mr Cecil was satisfied, and rose to go and get the medicine; but his physician pressed him to stay a little, and entered into conversation in a very fascinating style, till, engrossed with each other's company, the subject of the medicine was entirely set aside. On coming home, Mr Cecil expressed to his wife his admiration of his medical friend—'Such a fund of anecdote! such a command of language!' 'Well', exclaimed Mrs C, 'but did he prescribe for your case?' 'Yes—but I have entirely forgotten the remedy! the charms of his manner and conversation put everything else out of mind.' Now, we say, none of Mr Hammond's hearers ever are in danger of being thus carried away from the remedy to the eloquence, or the delivery, or any secondary matter in the address.

Another peculiarity is the use he makes of hymns. In all his meetings there is much hymn-singing, all of these hymns setting forth the truth. This hymn-singing attracts the young to the meetings; it rivets the truth on their minds; it adds greatly to the liveliness of the meetings. And is it not true that the only time in the New Testament wherein we find the worship of children noticed is that time when that worship consisted of praise—'The children crying in the temple, and saying, Hosanna to the Son of David'? (*Matt.* 21:15). The chief priests and scribes found fault;

their pharisaical pride would have thrust children into the background, but the Lord Jesus was filled with delight at the sound of their voices in the temple-courts.

Yet more. Mr Hammond never dismisses such a gathering hastily. After his pointed gospel-address is done, he prays, and then asks all to remain for conversation who are anxious to find salvation. He has always with him (this is a part of his method) a goodly number of solid and fervent Christians, who are ready to take part in these after-conversations. And this part of his method has been remarkably blessed; as much, indeed, as anything else in his dealing with the young. It is apparently very much by this conversational-meeting, in which you may see, all over the church or hall, lively believers engaged in most solemn inquiries with one or two souls whom the Spirit has touched, that very many are brought to decision. It seems to be the Holy Spirit's way to use this Nathan-like application of the truth to lead souls to own that the gospel is for themselves, and to admit, 'I am the sinner to whom the Saviour speaks.' The very circumstance, also, that so many at one time are earnestly engaged in the same solemn employment creates a healthful sympathy of feeling, and, in many cases, helps souls to utter their difficulties and fears.

We do not say that Mr Hammond's meetings have no drawbacks; but these are the features of his method which we might safely copy. And perhaps it ought to be stated that his labours have been specially useful in *bringing to decision* young persons who have long before been in an awakened state, through the instruction and prayers of teachers and parents, but who would never speak out their mind. He is greatly blessed to startle such, and bring on a crisis in their spiritual history.

Shall we not, then, with all these facts before us, ask the Church of Christ to cherish this expectancy in regard to the conversion of children far more than has been done in times past? Have we not leaned upon our oars? Have we not slipped into the custom of showing to our Sabbath Schools and families what a great and glorious salvation has been provided, and what a gracious and mighty Saviour is ours, without sufficiently urging them to make all this their own? We have dealt with the adults and with the aged earnestly, taking no excuse, but insisting on their immediate acceptance of Christ; but we have not been wont to deal thus also with the very youngest who can understand. If the Lord works by instrumentalities, and if it is by *suitable* instrumentalities, then let us see that we are taking the right way to bring blessing to the young. As a rule, the Lord does not convert souls in the absence of means, and in the absence of appropriate and right means. In heathen lands, souls perish because no one there shows to sinners the way of life. In our own neighbourhoods, men and women die unconverted, if no one goes among them seeking to win their souls. And so in our Sabbath-schools and families children grow up unconverted, because they are not more personally dealt with. Are we not *letting the souls of the young perish*, if we do not rouse ourselves to take part in this personal mode of applying the truth?

Lord, sharpen our sickles when we go to reap thy harvest among the young; for we have heard our Master say, 'Have ye not read, Out of the mouths of babes and sucklings thou hast perfected praise?'

12

ANGEL WORKERS

What I write is not a vision, nor a dream; it is an allegory of its kind. You will follow me into another region, to a spot where angels are gathered together in quiet, happy converse. They are 'all ministering spirits, sent forth to minister for them who shall be heirs of salvation' (*Heb.* 1:14); but they are creatures, and so they need intervals of rest. They, as well as we, find that 'iron sharpeneth iron'. Let me tell you my visit to one of these meetings, held under the shadow of that Throne whereon sitteth 'The Angel of the Covenant', who cared for Hagar, visited Abraham, wrestled with Jacob, spoke in the Burning Bush. On the right hand of that Throne, just where one arm of the emerald Rainbow dipt downward, a group of these ministering spirits were met to speak of the past, and to prepare for coming work. I got entrance into their circle, and they received me with great respect and glowing kindness, not for anything in myself, but for my work's sake and my Master's, I being on earth an 'Angel' of a Church of Christ, serving the same Lord whom they so loved and served.

Seated among them, I was allowed to listen and learn. Only a few spoke. It would have been most interesting to have heard anything from the two compassionate Angels who, in hurrying Lot and his family out of Sodom, taught us to 'pull men out of the fire'. But nothing fell from their lips, nor from any of the Mahanaim host (*Gen.* 32:2), who could have told of Jacob's timely comforts;

nor from the Angel who delivered Daniel from the lions; nor yet from the affable Angel with whom the Prophet Zechariah became so familiar. The notes I give, however, may be taken as recollections of what passed, in regard to things that concern us here below, in our sphere of service.

I.

The first who spoke was the irresistible Angel who, on the night of the Passover, was sent forth to destroy the firstborn of Egypt (*Exod.* 12:23; *Heb.* 11:28). He referred to that service as something very terrible, almost too terrible; but he was upheld by the discovery he got of the glory of divine justice in taking vengeance on sin. Glorious justice! how bright it shone forth in every stroke of his sword. Nor less was he revived when his eye from time to time turned to the blood-sprinkled lintels and door-posts of Israel, where grace was seen saving its thousands at the cost of divinely precious atonement, set forth in the blood of the Paschal Lamb. 'Angel of the Church of Finnieston (said he to me), tell your flock—never fail to tell and tell again—the justice of God, and, at the same time, the power of the blood which God has provided. Tell both unceasingly, that *the justice* may send souls to *the blood,* and our God be glorified in the highest, when 'a thousand fall at thy side and ten thousand at thy right hand', but the sword comes not nigh to those whose lintels and door-posts are sprinkled.'

II.

He sat down. And there stood up one like him in aspect, every way as majestic and mighty, yet very solemn and calm. It was the Angel who smote the host of Sennacherib, an hundred and eighty-five thousand in one night, using the drawn sword that once threatened death to Jerusalem (*1 Chron.* 21:16). He pictured the scene of exuberant and boisterous mirth in the Assyrian tents; their boastful exultation, as they fancied themselves already in the Temple; and then how the revelry died away, and sleep stole over them. How easy it was for him to go forth on his work! He needed only to flash his sword, and the heart of every sleeper was still for ever. 'But (said he) most dreadful was that scene of death, needing all the relief afforded by the blessed sight of believing Jerusalem at rest in the everlasting arms. As I passed Hezekiah's palace, how unutterably sweet it was to hear low-breathed words of calm confidence in our Jehovah! How peaceful were the dwellings of Jerusalem! O Angel of the Church of Finnieston, when you return, tell your flock what simple faith in our Jehovah wins. Tell anxious ones to look upon the blood of the mercy-seat, as did that king and his people, and use continually the appeal of simple faith.'

III.

When he had finished, another rose who prefaced what he was about to say by looking to me (as they all did, in their brotherly, familiar kindness) and stating who he was. 'I am the Angel who was sent to stop the false prophet Balaam on his way to curse Israel. It seemed a very small matter, scarcely requiring an Angel to be despatched from heaven to earth; but I joyfully went forth when my Lord called. And soon it appeared that had that man gone on to pronounce his withering curse, Israel would have had no courage to fight; Israel would not have entered the land; the promises to the seed of Abraham would have failed; Messiah would not have come; your world would have been unredeemed! Go and tell your flock the importance of a small service. Tell *parents* and *teachers* that to arrest evil, in the case of even one soul, may turn out to have been an inestimable blessing to the whole world.'

IV.

And now one rose who seemed the very ideal of angelic grace and kindness—the Angel who did that service, in the wilderness of Beersheba, to Elijah under the juniper-tree (*1 Kings* 19:5). He extolled the grace of his Lord and ours in delicately and tenderly reproving, while upholding, the desponding man of God. He rejoiced to relate how grace shone forth that day, when the peevishness of Elijah was twice requited by most seasonable refreshment, sent by him who would take no notice of his servant's infirmity in praying for death; for his God meant to take him up ere long to be Enoch's companion, without tasting death. When he had finished his brief story, his eye fell on me; and to me this message was entrusted, 'Angel of the Church of Finnieston, bid any who *work for the Lord, but who have become desponding,* and have thought of working no more because success seems to be so inadequate, bid them remember that day of which I speak. And see that thou thyself dost not lose temper with them; whereas thou shouldst rather carry to them, as I did to the prophet, the food and the water that will revive even a peevish worker's heart.'

V.

I saw next a mighty Angel prepare to speak, one whose name I soon learnt. But I should remark that for the most part I *could not catch the names of almost any.* They did not seem to care to be known individually by any one but their Lord. What a lesson (I thought) to some workers among us, who, unless they be spoken of, and their names made prominent, will not persevere in what they undertake. I saw there was no such sinful sensitiveness, no such ambition, in that holy heaven!

It was *Gabriel* who stood up now. With clear, full voice, that often quivered with joyous emotion, he told me of his privilege in being the messenger sent to Daniel, 'the man greatly beloved', to make known the time of the appearing of the Saviour, who was to finish transgression, make an end of sin, and bring in Everlasting Righteousness. With that eloquence that is peculiar (*1 Cor.* 13:1) to an angelic tongue, and to one who is high among them, 'standing before God', he went on to describe his second visit to earth on the same errand, when sent to the Temple of Jerusalem to announce the birth of Messiah's forerunner. But oh, how he was moved when next he related his mission to Nazareth, in which he announced to Mary that she was the mother of the Word made flesh! He did not, however, dwell upon his own feelings; the subject seemed too great even for him. 'But (said he ere he closed), Angel of the Church of Finnieston, we desire to look into your blessings, amid all our joys. O tell your *Elders,* and all among your flock who try to proclaim the love of God in sending his Son, that to us their privilege seems the highest that a creature can enjoy! To have such news to proclaim! It passes knowledge!'

VI.

Scarcely had he ended, when the subject was taken up by that favoured Angel who brought the tidings to the shepherds at Bethlehem, 'To you is born a Saviour, Christ, the Lord', while the glory of the Lord shone round about. 'Perhaps (he began) I may say my privilege was greater than Gabriel's, for I am the only one of our number who ever preached the gospel! Oh, it is sweet to sound the silver trumpet! When I was done with my brief message, how happy I thought the shepherds in being permitted to go everywhere and tell it all to their friends and neighbours. O Angel of a Church on earth, bid *all your flock* who know the ' Wonderful, the Mighty God, the Prince of Peace', go among their friends and neighbours as these shepherds gladly did. Nor forget to carry a word to those in your congregation who *lead the song*, and to all in the flock (for surely *they all join in the song*, every one), regarding the praise they offer. The multitude of the heavenly host, who joined me on that night almost ere I was done with my message, have often since declared that never did they find themselves so lifted up and blessed, as in singing to him who sent his Son, and singing with their eye on him who had come down to obey and suffer and die for sinners.'

He was about to close, when once more his eye fell on me, and he added, 'O son of man, you may have in your flock some who have your world's goods, which they might dedicate to their Lord and Saviour's use. A few days after that memorable night, when carrying a message to Joseph, who was still at Bethlehem (*Matt.* 2:19), I saw wise men who had been worshipping at the feet of Christ the Lord, who had gladly *offered gifts,* because their hearts were melted and moved and won at the sight of Incarnate Love. Use that argument, O man of God, whenever you would thaw the icy heart of any one among your flock who gives little to him who gave all for him. Tell your *Deacons* to use it, if they would open hearts; and let them enjoin their *Collectors* to employ this argument, which prevails when all others fail.'

VII.

A pause followed. I half expected to hear something from those Angels who 'came and ministered' to the Lord after the forty days' temptation. I hoped in my own mind that, in that case, I should have been able to tell at least the joy of our heavenly brethren not only in taking charge over us 'lest we dash our foot against a stone', but also in witnessing our success in times of temptation, when we overcome Satan 'by the blood of the Lamb and the word of his testimony'. But it seemed as if they were afraid lest we should look to them for the ministry of refreshment in hours of trial, rather than to the Holy Ghost, whose it is to anoint the overcomers 'with the oil of gladness'. As I was thus musing, one began to speak in whose utterance was an indescribable solemnity. He told of what work he had done on earth. This was the Angel who had strengthened the Lord Jesus in his agony in Gethsemane (*Luke* 22:43). 'O Angel of yonder Church on earth (said he), say to your *Communicants*—If they had been there! if they had seen one of the great drops of blood that fell on the cold ground! or one tear on that holy countenance, so marred and worn more than any man's! or had heard one groan, as he cried, "Abba, Father, if it be possible, let this cup pass from me!", they would surely come to the Communion-Table with awful reverence and wonder, their tears dropt into the cup of blessing, and the broken bread wet with the weeping of grateful love. Redemption money, what a price! Redeeming love, unfathomable! O Redeemer of men! for ever be honour and glory and blessing and thanksgiving to him that sitteth upon the throne, and to the Lamb!'

VIII.

By this time the fervour of the angelic assembly was gloriously intense. Everything about our Redeemer was evidently as interesting to them as to me. And forthwith the theme was continued; for the next speaker was the Angel who rolled away the stone from the door of the sepulchre (*Matt.* 28:2). 'I was bidden that morning put on the brightest robe in heaven, white as the snow, and my countenance was made to shine like the lightning, on which no man could gaze. I was to be employed in some very great work that day. Soon I learnt that what was required of me was to go down to your world, and in Joseph's garden, roll away a stone from the door of the sepulchre of your Lord and ours. Was this a work worthy of an Angel's powers, and of one so arrayed in glory? Angel of yonder Church on earth, tell your people that to do the least service to the Lord of glory is an inconceivable privilege and joy. Let it be known to your *Church-Officer*, let it be known to those who *'keep a door'* in God's house, as well as all who carry a *cup of cold water* to the sick, or *sew garments* for the poor, that no moment in my past life in heaven was to me half so sweet as was that time I sat on the rolled-away stone. I was rewarded by seeing him come forth, breaking the bands of death: a sight so glorious that no words could describe it to men. My task was very simple—the day before two men had rolled that stone to its place—and yet this was my reward! O the joy of working for the Lord of glory! O the bliss of being permitted to serve him in the commonest and easiest duty!'

IX.

I had no more than time to note down this message, when two, who had been sitting at my side, seemed as if they would like to speak. They were clothed in white raiment, and were very joyous. They seemed to me the 'Peter and John' of their company. Whether or not they were the same who were seen in the sepulchre of Christ, sitting, one at the head, the other at the feet where the body of Jesus had lain, I did not learn, though somehow I understood this to be the case. Both of these made as though they would have spoken; but one gave place to the other, and as he did so, whispered to me, 'Have not your feet stood on the Mount of Olives?' 'Yes', I said, 'and though it is now more than thirty years ago, I never can forget that hill and its olive trees.' 'And you were at Bethany too, and you will remember well the slope down the hill that leads to that favoured spot. It was there I and my brother angel stood on the day he is about to speak of.' Upon this I turned to listen; and that

other Angel told how on the day of the Ascension, just when the
wondrous procession was moving toward the Throne, and the glorified humanity of the Lord Jesus was beginning to light up heaven
with transcendent brightness—just when the interest and rapture
of the heavenly hosts had risen to a height beyond what was ever
known before—a sign was made to himself and his brother angel
to leave the hosts and turn down to earth, to the Mount of Olives,
that there they might deliver a brief message to eleven disciples,
sorrowing because their Master had been taken from their head,
at the moment when they had begun to hope that the Kingdom
he had told them to look for was about to appear. 'We were (he
added) for a moment startled; we almost fancied that this duty,
even if very urgent, might at any rate have been devolved on one
only, and that two need not have missed being present at that scene
which can never occur again in the history of the universe, when
the hosts of Angels and the redeemed around the throne witnessed
the Father's welcome to his beloved Son returning from redemption finished. O to have heard, 'Sit down at my right hand'! But tell
it on earth, O man of God, that forthwith we remembered his holy
will! Our rising regret was gone, and we went forth, our soul overflowing with delight, and with new and rarest joy. If any of your
flock be at times tempted to think hardly of their all-wise God
when he *detains them from the Sanctuary and the Communion-Table,*
let them know there is a joy quite peculiar and most satisfying
given to those who work for God in self-denying service, or who
can acquiesce in his ways. Forget not also to remind *all mourners*
that the tender sympathy of your Lord and ours is such that, amid
his own glory (glory above measure glorious!), and in the rapturous
hour of welcome to the right hand, he would comfort his sorrowing ones, and point them to the day when he shall return to wipe
away all tears. And not less plainly, also, did we see that day, the
Holy Ghost, the promised Comforter, in the greatness of his love,

anticipate the day of Pentecost, by letting fall some drops of the oil of gladness upon the bereaved disciples.'

X.

Excepting Gabriel (as I noticed before), no one of the assembly seemed to be marked out from each other by names. All were ready to serve unnoticed by their fellows. It was no wonder, therefore, that no name was given when the Angel who had been directed to go to Samaria, and send Philip away from that city to the road which led to Gaza (*Acts* 8:26), said a few things about that mission. 'I learnt again that day the deep lesson of Jehovah's sovereignty. Sometime before, one of our number, when he was sent to set free the twelve Apostles (*Acts* 5:19), was bidden tell them to 'Go and preach all the words of this life', but was not allowed himself to proclaim these words. And so it was in my own case now. I was not commissioned to give one ray of light to the Ethiopian eunuch in his sadness, but was simply bidden draw Philip away to a desert road, to meet one man, at a time when his hands were full of work in a crowded city. After delivering my message, I lingered near. The Spirit directed him to go up to the chariot, and explain to the Ethiopian inquirer the words about the Lamb led to the slaughter. O man of God, when you or any of your flock *are dealing with an anxious soul,* remember that day. All was still on the dusty road to Gaza; all was solemn and calm in the tone of Philip; there was deep earnestness, but no boisterous energy. He set forth the simple and clear truth about the Son of God who had come to be the sin-bearer. As he was telling the story of the God-man led as a lamb to the slaughter, 'the Just suffering for the unjust', it pleased the Holy Spirit to touch the heart of the Ethiopian; the scales fell from his eyes. He was filled with joy—and I hastened up to my place in heaven, to share the joy which fills the heavenly courts when one sinner repenteth.'

XI.

I now wondered in myself what might be the next word from the lips of these Angel workers. It was from the Angel who had been despatched to Jerusalem to open the prison and set Peter free. I cannot be sure that he was the same who carried the answer of prayer to Cornelius at Caesarea (*Acts* 10:3), though, somehow, I was led to think he was. However that may be, referring to both Cornelius and Peter, he did not fail, for my sake, to dwell upon the power of prayer, and the honour put upon it. 'Let the *Lord's remembrancers* know what we have been sent to do because they prayed. One man at Caesarea prayed and was heard. At Jerusalem, a little band united in the cry (*Acts* 12: 5, 7, 13); and let *the youngest* be often reminded that that little maid Rhoda's believing expectation was of no small importance in winning the answer.' Had time permitted, he would have gone on; and would probably have told about his being sent to complete the answer to the prayer, by cutting off proud Herod in the noon-day of his pride.

XII.

There was evidently an understanding among the gathered Angels that their hour of conference was near a close. But they were all desirous, in the exuberance of their brotherly love, that I should listen to Michael the Archangel, the leader of their host, whose very name is his banner, and declares his burning zeal for his Lord: for his name signifies, 'Who is like God?' On rising to close the meeting, he made allusion to events in his past errands to our world, such as his contending with the Devil for the body of Moses, the man of God; but instead of dwelling on any of these, took up another theme. His Lord and ours had made known to him a great work in prospect, which was ever present to his thoughts, viz., not only that he was to stand up for Israel in the Latter Day (*Dan.* 12:1), but that he should be sent, to our world, to sound the Last Trumpet at the Coming of Christ (*1 Thess.* 4:16). 'What a day (said he) that will be! O man of God, think often and much about it, as I do, and lead others to think on it much. You will forget all toil and weariness and care and trial on that day! The workers among you, the sowers who went out weeping, bearing precious seed, shall then have their day of reaping, and their bosom filled with sheaves. The trumpet shall sound, and the Son of God shall speak (*John* 5:25), and the dead in Christ shall rise, and the living saints be changed—a multitude whom no man can number, in resurrection-glory, and strength, and beauty, bearing the image of the heavenly! There are many mansions in New Jerusalem; and my brother Angel here, who once led the beloved John through New Jerusalem, declares that such is the glory of the place that he scarcely wondered when the bewildered disciple fell twice at his feet as if he would worship him. "Eye hath not seen, nor ear heard, nor has it entered the heart of man, what your God has prepared for those that wait for him." The city he has prepared for them is worthy of the God of grace and of glory. Angel of yonder Church on earth, hasten on to that day, and call on all your flock to hasten unto it, looking for the City, whose builder and maker is God, and for the Bright Morning Star. We are to be with him when he comes down to you that day; we are to gather his elect from the four winds, and then stand round you, beholding the glory and the rapturous joy, and joining in your Songs of Jubilee. Peace, peace be with you till that hour, when we shall meet again. The time is not revealed; "of that day and hour knoweth no man, neither the Angels in heaven." We understand, indeed, that now it is very near; but it shall come as a thief. Meanwhile, my beloved brother, be "steadfast, immovable, always abounding in the work of the Lord, inasmuch as you know that your labour is not in vain in the Lord."'

13

PRAYER AND FASTING

A Lecture on Daniel 10

The first verse of chapter ten says that Daniel's name was 'Belteshazzar', sending us back to the beginning of this book. When he was first brought to Babylon, his name was changed from Daniel to 'Belteshazzar', and very much has passed since then.

The events of this chapter happened seventy-two years after the first remarkable discovery that God made to Daniel in chapter 2. Daniel is now in his 90th year,—an old man, like John in Patmos.

The Lord delights in his people. He does not weary of them; he says, 'Even to your old age I am He; even to hoar hairs will I carry you'. 'I am He'—the very same. 'I have made, and I will bear; even I will carry and will deliver you.' He had done this with Daniel for more than seventy years, and now he comes to give Daniel a more remarkable discovery of himself than he has had in all his past years.

Old saints should take encouragement from this view of God's dealing with his servants. He does not let them faint or fail; 'They shall still bring forth fruit in old age: they shall be fat and flourishing.' Of all who are planted in God's soil this is true: every plant planted by God shall bring forth fruit in old age. If you are thus planted you shall not faint or fail, but, ever drawing your nourishment from the same rich soil, your roots getting deeper and deeper into it, you shall go on bearing fruit even in old age.

To young saints, also, there is encouragement from Daniel's history. He was early in God's service. He was eighteen when we first hear of him taking his stand on God's side. He was kept by God from that time on for seventy-two years,—kept from blemish,—kept from defiling himself with the things of the world, though living in the palace among the most wicked people. Young believers, take encouragement from Daniel's history. He who kept him can keep you. Go on trusting in him, saying, 'I will go in the strength of the Lord.'

But now let us fix our attention on this singular day in Daniel's experience. I do not know if there is a remarkable day—some day ever after to be remembered—in every believer's experience; but we do read of many such in the lives of Christians. John Howe has recorded such a day when he got a most overwhelming discovery of the grace and glory of the Saviour. We are told by Flavel, that going on a journey, he asked that it might not be a profitless journey, and that he might meet with nothing to interrupt his enjoyment of communion with God. The Lord made such wonderful discoveries of his grace, filling him on that day so full of gladness in him with whom he had fellowship, that he slipped from his horse on the green grass, and lay there prostrate till he awoke to find blood flowing from his nostrils. When he came to the house, he went at once to his room, afraid lest anything should come in to interrupt the joy of which his heart was still full. The next day the glory had passed by; but he never forgot what he had experienced; it helped him all his journey through. It may be the Lord will so deal with saints in our day, also. But do we wait on him?

Notice in this chapter—

1st. Daniel *at the Passover time.*

2nd. Daniel *in prayer at the Passover time.*

3rd. Daniel *on the old site of Paradise.*

4th. Daniel *like John in Patmos.*

1. *Daniel at the Passover Time.*

It says here: 'In the four-and-twentieth day of the first month',— that was the month Abib, the Passover month. It is worth noticing this. He spent three full weeks in his fasting and prayer; that was considerably more than the time of the Passover feast, which continued only seven days. He took in a little on both sides of the Passover time,—a few days before, and a few days after. He could not go to Jerusalem. He saw it his duty to remain where he was; like Nehemiah, who saw it his duty to remain most of his time with the king his master. Daniel remained at Babylon, taking care of the interests of God's people there, and shining in the palace. Still, his heart was at Jerusalem. Three times a day he opened the window of his chamber toward Jerusalem, and prayed. He could say,—if we could have listened below his window we might have heard him say,—'If I forget thee, O Jerusalem, let my right hand forget her cunning. If I do not remember thee, let my tongue cleave to the roof of my mouth, if I prefer not Jerusalem above my chief joy'. He well remembered that at this season the tribes were going up to Jerusalem to keep Passover there. He could not be there in the body, but his heart was there. He knew that he needed the blood of the Paschal Lamb as much as they.

Can we all say with as true a heart as Daniel, 'If I forget thee, O Jerusalem, let my right hand forget her cunning'? Can you ever forget Calvary? Can you forget the great, the true Paschal Lamb there offered? have you not need of the blood shed there?

Let us not fail to notice that Daniel was interested in the Passover-offering in his old age. It has not lost its value in his eyes. He did not say; 'I am a saint of threescore years and ten, and do not need the Paschal blood.' No; he needs it still, even more than at the first.

Further, from his example, let us learn to sympathize with brethren. Do we sympathize with our brethren? 'Let brotherly love continue.' Take care of getting isolated, of being shut up, and having a heart only for a small circle. Seek to have a heart of love for all the brethren, because they love your Lord.

2. *Daniel in Prayer at the Passover Time.*

Verse 2: 'In those days I, Daniel, was mourning three full weeks. I ate no pleasant bread, neither came flesh nor wine in my mouth, neither did I anoint myself at all till three whole weeks were fulfilled.' Fasting meant nothing to the godly Israelite without prayer. Besides, his speaking to God is expressly mentioned in the 12th verse, 'Thy words were heard.' So it was a time of prayer as well as fasting. The fasting, the not eating pleasant meat, and the not anointing of himself,—all were in order to speed the prayer.

Daniel found time for much prayer, which every Christian does not. He made time. He was a man of business; and, let it be noted, though every man of business does not find time for prayer, yet Daniel did. Yes, he found time for abundant prayer. He took the time; he would rather have let the business go than not get time for prayer: But he did not need to omit the one for the other; he found time for both. He was president over the 127 provinces of that vast empire of which we read. What an amount of work he must have had! But just because of this he says, 'I must pray.' Like Luther, of whom we are told that, when he had more than usual to do, he said that therefore he must have many more hours for prayer. A London city missionary remarked the other day, that we should not need to work so hard if we prayed more, for then the Lord to whom we pray would bring the work more easily to our hands. *We may have the same experience if we try.*

This president of 127 provinces finds time to pray in the midst of his business. Or perhaps he takes a holiday time? Do people in their holiday time pray the more,—do they grasp the holiday as a time for more abundant prayer? Do they not generally pray less on that day? Do they not say that they are out of harness from work, and make it a time when they are out of harness from prayer too?

Daniel did not so. The fasting, the giving up pleasant meat, and anointing himself, was just that he might not be entangled with anything that might hinder prayer during this season which he had set apart for it. If, when you go aside from the world for prayer, you find food, or anything else, entangle you and hinder your prayer, give it up. It may not be food, it may be your ordinary reading or some common occupation,—but whatever it may be that entangles you and keeps you from prayer, give it up for the time. If you find giving up food weakens you and hinders you in prayer, fasting in that case is not good for you. But it is good for many of us, and the Lord Jesus said, 'The days shall come, when the Bridegroom shall be taken away from them, and then shall they fast in those days.' Are not our days the time when the Bridegroom is still absent from us? We are still waiting for his return.

Daniel spent his fasting time in prayer, and he did it with his eye on the Paschal Lamb, which at that very time was being offered up in Jerusalem.

But notice what we discover in verse 13, viz. that *if you set yourself to pray much, Satan will set himself to hinder you.* 'The prince of the kingdom of Persia withstood me one and twenty days',—which was just all the time that Daniel's prayer was going on. The Lord was listening, and the devil tried to prevent him from listening,—tried to get him to shut his ears to Daniel's strong cry. If you go apart for a time of prayer, the devil will try to interrupt you, and stop you in your prayer; but that just shows its value. And remember, when you pray, and Satan tries to hinder, the great Intercessor takes up the case, and he must prevail. He says, *'Fear not, Daniel; for from the first day* that thou didst set thine heart to understand, and to chasten thyself before thy God, *thy words were heard,* and I am come for thy words.'

3. Daniel on the Old Site of Paradise.

'I was by the side of the great river, which is Hiddekel.' That 'great river', so deep and broad, which, from its source in the mountains, flows 1,100 miles, has for us a special interest, for it was one of the rivers of Paradise,—one of the first rivers mentioned in the Bible, where, in Genesis 2, it is mentioned along with Pison, and Gihon and Euphrates as flowing through the garden of Eden. This Hiddekel, otherwise named Tigris, flowed along within the bounds of the old Paradise.

It seems probable that Daniel had come to the old site of Paradise purposely at this Passover time, there to spend his holiday as a time of prayer. Perhaps he had an estate there; he may have bought one in that spot because of its old associations. There he walks, meditating and praying by the side of 'that ancient river' Hiddekel. What thoughts it would bring up! Here (he would remember) is where our first parents walked with God, and held communion with him! Here also they sinned, and their communion with God was broken up! Here Adam tried to hide himself from God amid the trees of the garden. What views of sin he would get as he thought of all this! Here is where Adam fell! Here (near this at least) must that tree have stood whence he plucked the forbidden fruit. Not far off from here must be the spot where the Cherubim were placed, and where the Flaming Sword shut him out from his Paradise. What has sin done! What a change and blight have come over this earth since our first parents dwelt here in peace and joy! What a contrast now! Paradise and Babylon! Holiness and bliss; corruption and its fruits! We can suppose how thoughts of the Fall would rise naturally in the mind of Daniel, as he walked by the side of Hiddekel. But he would have other thoughts than of sin and lost communion with God. He would say; Through the blood of the Paschal Lamb, which they are now offering in Jerusalem, I get back communion with God; I have all my sin blotted out, and can meet with him who met with Adam here, and walked with him.

Do we often thus go back to the fountain of sin and corruption? Do we sometimes take the words of the 51st Psalm, and say, 'Behold, I was shapen in iniquity, and in sin did my mother conceive me'? Do we go back in thought to Paradise, and mourn with Adam and Eve over the eating of the forbidden fruit? Let us call to mind our share in the sin of the world. What a view of the virulence of sin does it give us, when we think that the sin of Adam has gone down through all their descendants, is still working such terrific havoc in the world around us!

But while we think of this, let us not forget that the lost communion can be restored, because he came who was the 'Seed of the woman'. Somewhere yonder (Daniel would say) did God speak the first promise. And you today can think of that promise as fulfilled in Christ, and can claim for yourself the Seed of the woman.

Once more: observe that the result of these twenty-one days of fasting and prayer was something well worth waiting for. While Daniel is by the Hiddekel, he sees some one walking towards him among the trees that border the river. Is it old Adam, of whom he had been thinking? No, it is the Second Adam, and that is better than the First; for notice now,

4. *Daniel, like John in Patmos,*

in the discovery made to him of the Lord Jesus. This was God's way of rewarding him for those days of waiting. 'Then I lifted up mine eyes, and looked, and behold a certain Man clothed in linen', fine linen, always the symbol of righteousness—'whose loins were girded with fine gold of Uphaz',—the golden ephod: this is one not only spotless in righteousness, but priestly too. 'His body also was like the beryl', or chrysolite, indicating the bright yet mild splendour of his person. 'And his face as the appearance of lightning'—too glorious to be gazed on steadily, as in the Transfiguration. 'And his eyes as lamps of fire',—he can see others though they cannot gaze on him. 'And his arms and his feet like in colour to polished brass',—he has perfect purity, that takes on no soil of earth, though it treads this world; just as he could touch a leper, not taking on leprosy, but destroying it. 'And the voice of his words like the voice of a multitude',—like the 'sound of many waters', as John says. You can see at once that this is the Son of Man.

At first, the vision was overpowering. Daniel says, 'There remained no strength in me'; and again, verse 17, 'Neither is there breath left in me.' His bodily frame suffered under the overpowering vision of glory; but the special reference of the words is to the feelings of the soul. 'I saw him, and knew what I was by comparison. If I had had a self-complacent thought before, it was gone now; my comeliness was turned in me into corruption.' Like Isaiah (*Isa.* 6:5), when he beheld the Lord in vision, 'Then said I, Woe is me, for I am undone; because I am a man of unclean lips.'

The sight of the Lord Jesus always has this effect on the believer. It strips a man of all self-righteousness and self-complacency, and leaves him overwhelmed with the feeling of utter vileness and nothingness. The nearer you get to the Saviour, you will, by comparison, see the more of your own loathsomeness, and will abhor yourself the more. By looking into yourself, and dwelling on the evils of your own heart, you may find out something of the sin within you; but, while you may go a long way in finding out the corruption within you, you may, at the same time, come to be very self-complacent over your own clearness of vision in the matter, and may feed your corruption on your corruption. On the other hand, come near Christ, and in the twinkling of an eye you are emptied of all self-complacency, and are down in the dust in self-abhorrence, and a sense of your own nothingness. Of all ways the most thorough, to make a man humble and self-abased, is for him to see in the light of Christ what he is in himself.

Another effect of the vision on Daniel was, he 'became dumb'. No wonder that the glory of the Son of man thus seen, should make him dumb with awe and wonder. But all this was a preface to something better still; for here was a discovery not only of the glory, but also of *the grace of the Son of man*. 'When I heard the voice of his words, then was I in a deep sleep on my face.' It is curious that the word used here is the same word as that used in Paradise (*Gen.* 2:21) when a 'deep sleep' fell on Adam, and the Lord took the rib from his side and made of it a woman. It was no doubt a refreshing sleep,—a sleep that was to prepare him for the vision.

Then we are told, 'An hand touched me',—a human hand. As in Patmos, when John saw the vision, he says, 'I fell at his feet as dead, and he laid his right hand upon me, and said, Fear not'; so here the Lord says to Daniel, 'O Daniel, a man greatly beloved, . . . Fear not, Daniel.' You see here the grace of Christ, and how sweet it is to see that his grace is no new thing in him. We see it fully in New Testament days, but he was the same to the Old Testament saints. How sweet to know that love and grace in the bosom of the Son of man were the same in their deep fountain when he was in the bosom of the Father, before he came forth to manifest himself in his humanity! Let us study Christ's heart more: it draws us so close to him. Let us study his words. Hear how he speaks to Daniel,—'A man greatly beloved', a 'man of desires'. O man of God, do you believe that the Lord has intense as well as real desire towards you? When you go to meet him at his Table, or at the mercy-seat, he is there before you, as one that loves you so much that he could not stay away. 'As the Father hath loved me, so have I loved you' (*John* 15:9).

And recollect that he whose grace is manifested here is seen as Priest, to assure us that he was quite able to meet us sinners. He is a Priest: he has the hyssop and the blood ready to wash away all defilement. When he comes to hold communion with me, he comes as one who will see all that is in me, but who, in that same moment, whatever spot or stain of sin is on me, wipes it away. Thus he can hold communion with us in a holy fellowship, and we may say to him, 'Let him kiss me with the kisses of his mouth: for thy love is better than wine.'

O what grace is here! And such (may I not say) is the reward of waiting closely on the Lord in earnest, continued prayer. You will get discoveries of Christ in his glory, and grace, such as you have never yet had. If you set yourself to wait on the Lord, the Second Adam will meet you, and reveal himself to you. He may meet you to humble you,—to lay you in the very dust in self-abhorrence and abasement,—to empty you of every thought of self-satisfaction. If so, all the better; because, when he does thus humble you and empty you, it is to prepare you for further usefulness. Daniel was thus humbled that afterwards he might have new employment in God's service. 'When he had spoken to me, I was strengthened.' If he empties, it is in order to fill; if he weakens, it is that he may afterwards supply new strength. After Daniel is thus strengthened, he gets a communication made to him by the Son of man as the Prophet of his people. He was pleased to reveal to his servant much of the history of the world's kingdoms, on through the centuries to come, even to the time when 'many of them that sleep in the dust of the earth shall awake', and when 'they that turn many to righteousness shall be as the stars for ever and ever.'

Remember, when the Lord did this for Daniel, he did it as the response to that waiting on him in these weeks of fasting and prayer. When Isaiah was humbled under the sense of his vileness, and then was lifted up with a fresh sense of forgiveness, he sent him to a new work (*Isa.* 6:8-9). And there will be some such results for us too, if we meet with the Lord, and, being emptied of all self-strength and complacency, are anew filled with his grace and strength.

There is a lesson of another kind here for those who may not be interested in the subject of our meditation. The men who were with Daniel when he beheld this vision hid themselves. They fled, and so did not behold the glory of the vision; they were themselves to blame for their not seeing the sight. Perhaps, if they had remained, the Lord would have revealed himself to them also. If you do not get the discovery of the Lord that others do, it is your blame: you have gone away from him, you have hid yourself from him. And it is well to observe, the Lord suffered them to go away: nor did he compel them to come back—he let them go. So it may be with you; the blame being all your own for remaining out of the way.

But once more. There is not a simpler or more effectual way of learning much of sin in its hatefulness and loathsomeness, and the working of it in us, than this of coming into the presence of Christ, waiting on him in prayer and fasting. Draw near to him; invite him to come near to you, to show himself evidently to you in his glory and his grace,—and so you will see what sin is, and what you are. There is not a better way of learning the whole truth than this of coming into the presence of the Lord, and dwelling for a season under his eye, inviting the blessed Potter to mould the softened clay.

14

THE GREAT GIVER
TEACHING TO GIVE

Believing men are to be not merely cisterns, but springs. 'He that believeth on me, out of him shall flow rivers of living water' (*John* 7:38). One of these rivers which the Master declared should not fail to flow from his believing ones is delight in giving, or the gladsome habit of using all we possess as stewards for the Lord, and not as proprietors of the same. When an Israelite had offered the sacrifice of atonement at the altar, he must forthwith thereafter bring the *mincha*, or meat-offering, an offering in which he symbolically gave up to the Lord the possession of all his property. But we should not have said, 'he must bring'; for it was all privilege—he was permitted to bring his property, to give vent to his gratitude, to exhibit practically, 'What shall I render to the Lord for all his benefits?' So did Zacchaeus at Jericho; so did the Pentecostal Church at Jerusalem.

Many do not seem to notice how often the Lord Jesus inculcated truth regarding this matter. His sayings on the point are very many; nor do we wonder that it should be so, considering that selfishness is in us a root of bitterness ever springing up to trouble us.

1. *He stated the Duty.* And when he did so, it was done in startling terms. We read in Luke 6:30, '*Give to every one that asketh of thee.*' Have we read the words aright? Yes, the words are plain. Is there no other translation possible? No, they are too plain and

downright to admit of any doubt. Is there no various reading, then? No, none; the words stare you in the face, *'Give to everyone that asketh of thee'!*

Disciples of Christ, you are to be a Light, ever dispensing rays; you are to be a Well, affording something to all who come. As you are to 'Pray without ceasing', and to 'Give thanks in everything' (*1 Thess.* 5:17, 18), so you are to have an always-giving heart and hand—a realization of that Well over which was written:

> Christian reader view in me,
> An emblem of true charity,
> Who freely what I have bestow,
> Though neither heard nor seen to flow;
> And I have full returns from heaven,
> For every cup of water given.

While another, who is not a disciple, may be grumbling, 'So many calls!' you are to reply, 'Yes, very many; but they are all calls in providence to cultivate in me a giving disposition.' The Master had very 'many calls' upon him for healing all disease, and helping all want, and *'gave to everyone'.*

Let us understand the context of this passage, Luke 6:30. In the preceding verses, Christ inculcates, 'Love your enemies, do good to them that hate you, bless them that curse you, pray for them that despitefully use you' (*Luke* 6:27, 28). This is the very mind that was in him; this was what the Cross exhibited to the full; this is the heart of the gospel, which is truly the manifestation of God's love to enemies in the Beloved Son, made a curse for sinners that he might bless them. And surely this is the holy mind that disciples are expected to copy from their Master. Then in verse 29, we see the meekness and calmness of Christ: 'Unto him that smiteth thee on the one cheek offer also the other: and him that taketh away thy cloak forbid not to take away thy coat also.' We, his disciples, are expected to possess a meekness of spirit and a self-control that would carry us this length, whenever circumstances required. And so verse 30 comes in: 'Give to every one that asketh of thee'; followed by the clause: 'And of him that taketh away thy goods, ask them not again.' Surely these are words that call for a giving mind, and a readiness to let go the things that are lawfully ours! Can less than this be the meaning?

If, then, we turn to Matthew 5:39-42, we have the same subject treated of in very similar terms. It bids us not revenge, but be prepared 'if one smite us on one cheek, to offer also the other'—not revenge but rather, 'if compelled to go a mile, go two', should that be the alternative,—not revenge but if unjustly dealt with so that 'one sue thee at the law and take away thy coat, let him have thy cloak also'—far better to adopt this alternative than exhibit the spirit of the world. Even so, *'Give to him that asketh of thee,* and from him that would borrow of thee, turn not thou away', calls upon us to be ever ready to give, instead of being annoyed, as some are by 'so many calls'. When asked, or when providence puts a case in our way, there must be no harsh denial, but at least an entire willingness to give, if a case of need be apparent.

In all this, who can fail to discern the spirit and tone of the Lord Jesus, whose charity sought not its own, but laid out even glory itself on us the undeserving? Such a tone of character, therefore, must be essential to real holiness, and the want of it a deformity, inasmuch as such a want is unlikeness to the Lord.

> Give strength, give thought, give deeds, give pelf,
> Give love, give tears, and give thyself;
> Give, give—be always giving,
> Who gives not, is not living,
> The more we give,
> The more we live.

2. *He stated the Manner.* We are to give with a happy, cheerful feeling, as being privileged to do a blessed thing. 'It is more
blessed to give than to receive' (*Acts* 20:35) are words of the Lord
Jesus—words preserved and embalmed in the Church, words so
well known that Paul could refer to them as in a manner prover-
bial, words that bear the peculiar and unmistakable characteristics
of the soul and heart of him from whose lips they fell. They are
words that tell us not simply that 'God loveth a cheerful giver' (*2
Cor.* 9:7), but that God has connected blessedness with right giving, so that the giver's face cannot fail to shine, if he knows what
he is doing. Yes, *'It is more blessed to give'*, as Mary did at Bethany,
'than to receive', as Solomon did when his ships returned laden with
gold of Ophir, and every rare and precious thing.

Giving, it appears, is not to be reckoned self-denial at all. It
would have been no wonder though the Lord had made this call
on us for giving, even if every act of giving had been sore self-
denial, a wrenching off a right hand. But it turns out that there is
no self-denial in it to a soul fully imbued with the mind of God.
To such a soul, 'It is more blessed to give than to receive.' We do
no one a favour by our giving; we bless ourselves; that is, we, in the
very act, break open the alabaster box which pours on ourselves its
fragrance and refreshing.

The grand illustration of this blessedness is to be found in the
Godhead. Man likes to get, God likes to give; and it is God that
is 'blessed for ever'. In the plan of Redemption, we find the Father
counting it 'more blessed to give than to receive'. He develops (so
to speak) his own bliss by giving that immense, that infinite gift,
his own Son. This is the rate at which he, whose blessedness is giving, delights to give. Here is a gratification of the giving heart; he
bestows on man the unspeakable gift, the beloved Son. To him he
grants the gift of a multitude that no man can number, a countless
flock of ransomed souls for their shepherd's glory, while to each

of the flock he gives not only the beloved Son, but also the Holy Spirit with all his stores of graces and of joys. Then, also, we find the *Son's* rate of giving to be in no respect less liberal. He gives himself, 'God manifest in flesh', for us, himself with all his obedience, all his suffering and death, all his merit, and all that all these purchase and make sure. The price of the purchased blessings must not be forgotten; for he gave not only service, but anguish, woe, death, in short, whatever justice sought—all in order to present us with grace and glory, without money or price on our part. O what giving is this! O my soul, what giving is here! And the Holy Ghost, also (who in *Psa.* 51:12, is called 'the free', i.e., the princely, or generous, or liberal Spirit) comes in the name of Jesus, and makes a gift of himself! so that thus in one sum we are made to receive, 'Love, joy, peace, goodness', in short, all holiness, all excellency, and all that is contained in Eternal Life. What giving! we again exclaim. The full sea of Godhead-bliss flowing in upon man! And this giving is one of the forms of Godhead felicity. 'It is more blessed to give than to receive.' Men and brethren, who would not taste something of this peculiar joy? 'It is not your money I want (says a man of God), but your happiness.'

3. *He stated the Measure, and Rule.* 'Freely ye have received, freely give' (*Matt.* 10:8). Ye have got from your Master without his looking for requital in any shape; give ye to your fellow-men without regard to the probability of requital from them. This is so far the force of *'freely'*; but add to this also the amount of what we received freely from him. Who can forget how full, how frank, how generous he was! The pattern of our giving as to measure is to be *the Lord's own* measure; and in regard to that we know that he gave as prompted by his own loving, kindly, generous nature; not stinting the amount by regard to the likelihood of getting thanks or meeting with a return of benefit. Let none, therefore, excuse in himself an unreadiness to give by saying , 'Possibly, it may be

turned to little advantage by the person who gets'—that word 'Freely', enjoins you to copy the Saviour's example; to open wide your heart and hand even though your kindness be ill-requited, or never owned at all. Neither say, 'I have stopped giving in the meantime, because others, equally able, are not giving up to their measure.' What hast thou to do with what other men give? We ask again, what hast thou to do with what other men give? Thy part is to remember and to consider *what thou hast received;* yes, what *thou thyself* (leaving others out of view) *hast received at the hand of God.* Look at the largeness of that amount, and how it was given, unstinted and ungrudged, in spite of his knowledge of selfishness in thee, selfishness which (like the sand drinking in the rain) would so quickly appropriate all, and exhale upward almost nought. M'Cheyne quotes the saying of an old Divine: 'What would have become of us if Christ had been as saving of his blood as some men are of their money?'

And farther. When Jesus says, *'Ask and it shall be given you'* (*Matt.* 7:7; *Luke* 11:9), does he not suggest much as to the measure; especially when he adds, 'What man of you is there whom if his son ask bread, will he give him a stone? or if he ask a fish, will he give him a serpent?' The measure here is simply, *the very thing required.* Christ gives not merely something but up to the supplying of the want; if we copy him here, then as far as lies in our power we shall aim at giving as much as will meet the exigency, as much as will come up to the demand. You know that we are only *stewards* of all we possess; our money is not our own. 'Occupy till I come' is the superscription on every coin.

But reverting again to Matthew 10:8, *'Freely ye have received, freely give',* let us notice that the first application of that counsel was in reference to the preaching of the gospel, the imparting to other men what they themselves had received. Go and tell your fellow-men these good news, however ungratefully hearers of it may act towards you; for you yourselves were undeserving of such a blessing when the Lord sent it. Show your estimate of what you have received by your efforts to impart it to others far and wide. Do this by personally telling it as opportunity occurs, faithfully, frequently, prayerfully.

But since you can do it very effectually (and far more extensively than your personal influence can reach) by helping others to proclaim the tidings of great joy, you must not, you cannot, fail to avail yourselves of this means of *'freely giving'*. What, then, is the rate of your giving for the support of the gospel ordinances at home? Is it such that you can say: 'You may fairly estimate my sense of the value of the gospel by the measure of my giving'? We do not ask, Do you give ten shillings annually toward the support of the Ministry, or do you give ten pounds? but ask, Is your giving such in its measure that God could point to it and say, 'See! here is one who gives freely, because he feels that he received freely!' As to our spreading the gospel among the Jews and the heathen—what a melancholy calculation that is which was recently made in regard to the communicants of two of the most numerous Presbyterian bodies in this land, viz.: that the yearly average of Missionary giving for every communicant amounted to somewhat like one shilling and no more! As if each communicant said, 'I value my share in the gospel at this rate. I give at the rate at which I received!' Shall the Lord judge any of us by this measure? Has he deserved no more than this at our hands?

4. *He stated some of the Benefits resulting.*

These are his words: *'Give and it shall be given unto you; good measure, pressed down and shaken together and running over, shall men give into your bosom. For with the same measure that ye mete, it shall be measured to you again'* (*Luke* 6:38). Here is a promise of recompense, ay, of recompense for doing what is in itself most blessed! For such is the Lord's manner. How like him who said: 'Whosoever shall give to drink to one of these little ones a cup of cold water only, in the name of a disciple, verily I say unto you, he shall in no wise lose his reward' (*Matt.* 10:42). 'Blessed is he that considereth the poor, the Lord will deliver him in the time of trouble' (*Psa.* 41:1). It was the same Lord who by the mouth of David said: 'I have not seen the righteous forsaken, nor his seed begging bread: he is ever merciful and lendeth, and his seed is blessed'—where (you see) the giving characteristic of the man thus blessed is unmistakably held up to view. It is not every good or righteous man; it is the generous, the 'lending', righteous man. And how truly in keeping with his own manner was that saying of the Master to the Young Ruler, 'Sell whatsoever thou hast and give to the poor, and thou shalt have treasure in heaven' (*Mark* 10:21).

In point of fact, men and brethren 'giving well' is as needful to our soul's prosperity as 'doing well'; and on the other hand, as surely as 'the doer of the work is blessed in his deed' (*James* 1:25), so surely is the willing giver of his substance blessed in his giving. Hearken, beloved brethren! 'Thy prayers and thine alms are come up as a memorial before God' (*Acts* 10:4). Hearken yet again: 'Not that I desire a gift, but I desire fruit that may abound to your account' (*Phil.* 4:17), is the language used respecting the giving of the jailor at Philippi, the givings of Epaphroditus, Lydia, Euodias, Syntyche, and the rest who had ministered of their substance to Paul.

It was the experience of a godly Glasgow merchant in other days, that the liberal man is the man whose riches are likely to continue with him. He quaintly remarked, in allusion to Proverbs 23:5, that 'clipping the wings' was the only way to prevent riches flying away as the eagle. There was deep meaning in his words; for the Master's words go thus far, and much beyond it, too. Notice the special terms of Christ's declaration; not only shall you get some requital, but you shall find 'good measure, pressed down, shaken together, and running over'! This is the recompense! What words are these! What a promise is here! The complete fulfilment shall soon reach us in the Kingdom, but oven here we shall often get instalments.[1]

And do you not think, brother, that you and I have good security for the loan which we may lend to the Lord?

A man says: 'I do wish to get blessing for the ministrations of my pastor and for gospel ordinances.' And this man prays for blessing as well as diligently attends on ordinances. But the man must add to his plan; he must also 'give', and not leave it to others to give all. He must have a hand in the sums gathered for upholding the ordinances, just as Cornelius had his 'alms' ready, as well as his 'prayers'. They who do not give according to their ability to the sustentation of the Ministry, need not expect to get the benefits they would otherwise obtain. 'Give, and it shall be given unto you.'

Another says: 'I wish the congregation I am connected with to flourish; its schools, its schemes of benevolence, and all such objects; I pray for them often and heartily.' Well, but Cornelius would have added 'alms' to 'prayers'. We do not shrink from saying, You must put into the plate of what God has given you, as well as put your prayer into the censer of the High Priest. 'Give, and it shall be given unto you.'

Another says: 'I am deeply interested in the cause of missions; I long for the day when Jew and Gentile shall all know the Lord.' But do you, besides good wishes and prayers, give the help of your money? Not the mere mite which you never feel the want of, but the sum that testifies that your interest is really deep and practical?

But one of our poor brethren puts in a question here. 'Am I, then, necessarily a loser under ordinances because I have not got

[1] Our version seems to convey the idea that the recompense is to be conveyed by the hands of men; *shall men give unto you* (*Luke* 6:38). But the Greek phrase signifies simply, 'It shall be given to you.' They whose business it is to do it shall be employed by God to give the over-running abundance of reward.

the means of giving, and so cannot bring an offering?' No, not at all; your case is of the same class with that of the sick and feeble, stretched on beds of languishing, who cannot work and labour for God, but have 'the will to do it'. The Lord knoweth the 'willing' heart and the willing one may rest assured that to him Jehovah is saying, as to David when he would fain have built the Temple and was not permitted (*1 Kings* 8:18), 'Thou didst well that it was in thine heart' (*2 Cor.* 8:12). Only be honest and true with God in the matter. Surely the man can work and labour in God's cause who can find time and strength for visiting friends and evening parties; so also the man is able to give much to God's cause who can 'spend' so largely on his family and domestic comforts, who can indulge himself in buying what is only a luxury, and who can lay up money in the bank less or more. At the same time, poor believer, all 'giving' is really 'sowing'; and you are a gainer by giving your few shillings. 'A handful of seed sown may yield great increase.'

Man of God, let us ask the great Giver to teach us to give!

Anxious, unsatisfied soul, there are some whose *secret unhappiness* goes hand in hand with their want of a generous tone of mind. These persons are not able to discern the large-hearted grace of God; they judge God by themselves; their narrow hearts represent God as one who gives indeed, but gives sparingly, or conditionally, or in consideration of previous desert. Were your soul more generous in its tone, you might be better able to discern the generous freeness and fullness of God's giving; but a withholding, miserly soul is too likely to picture to itself a withholding God, who must be repaid for his gifts, and from whom blessings must be wrung by making out a claim. May the Holy Ghost give you a true discovery of our God who 'giveth to all men liberally and upbraideth not' (*James* 1:5).

Unsaved man; perhaps you are liberal and benevolent. You give well, because your natural disposition is amiable and kind; but you do not, in your givings even to religious objects recognise Christ. If so, you will yet hear him say; 'You did it not to me' (*Matt.* 25:45); you gave either to enjoy the luxury of complacent self-applause, or because you felt it pleasant to see others pleased. Brother, in such giving the Lord Jesus takes no pleasure. Benevolence, charity, liberality, generosity, wash no sins away and form no righteousness. Will ye listen to us when we invite your attention to the delight which the Lord Jesus has in your receiving from him? Jesus would fain give Eternal Life—pardon, peace, purity, glory—to such undeserving ones as you, who make a righteousness out of your givings to men, and are withholding your conscience from the cleansing blood and your heart from his holy fellowship.

Perhaps, unsaved man, you may belong to another class—those who refuse to give a mite to religious objects, and who cry out about neglecting the poor at home. You say it is all waste to spend money on gospel ordinances, on missions, and the like, though Jesus commended and rewarded the woman who spent ten pounds, in order to anoint his head (*Matt.* 26:10-13). Well, here is the truth as to you; you give nothing to Christ because you know him not. You set no value on perishing souls, because your own soul is unsaved. You have never seen your state of sin and death, and how near to the brink of perdition you stand at this hour. You have never understood the free love of God, nor seen his glory. But stay, unsaved man; what voice is that which reaches our ears? 'What is a man profited, if he gain the whole world and lose his own soul?' (*Matt.* 16:26.) Do you not know that the love of money is the love of sin —ay, that thy money shall perish with thee—and that thou shalt be so poor in eternity as not to be able to get one drop of water? One thing, however, let us not fail to tell you: a man enthralled to earth, to self, to sin, to Satan, may he delivered from them all, if he make haste. For the Holy Spirit sets free the soul by revealing Christ that died and rose again. This is the sight, this is the sun, that melts an earth-worm's and a miser's heart. The cross is still as powerful as when Paul said, that it was by it 'the world was crucified to him and he unto the world' (*Gal.* 6:14). It is still as truly 'the power of God' as when Cowper sung of it:

> It was the sight of Thy dear cross,
> First weaned my soul from earthly things,
> And taught me to esteem as dross
> The mirth of fools and pomp of kings.

15

THE CLOAK LEFT AT TROAS

Reading Paul's words in 2 Timothy 4:13, 'The cloak which I left at Troas with Carpus, when thou comest, bring with thee, and the books, but especially the parchments', some have asked, Did the Holy Ghost dictate these words to his servant? Our reply is, Beyond all doubt it was the Holy Spirit, and not merely Paul, that put these common words into an inspired epistle; for no man of himself would have imagined that a circumstance apparently so trivial should have formed a clause in a letter written under the dictation of the Holy Ghost. And when we calmly sit down to consider it, we soon see that there are many lessons taught us. See here,

1. *God's Sympathy with the Privations of his People.* He loved Paul (*Gal.* 2:20); and this being the case, not one concern of his but is interesting to God. There is not a hair of Paul's head but is numbered; not a step but is ordered; not a wandering but is noted down; not a tear but is in his book. And so, he bids him tell Timothy about 'the cloak' left at the house of Carpus, in Troas. It concerns Paul's comfort; therefore (says the Holy Spirit,) write about it, and let all men know that our God (the Holy Spirit as well as Jesus) is so loving and so great (*Job* 36:5) that he can interest himself in the minutest affairs of his people. If they be shivering in the cold, he thinks on their uncomfortable state, and sends relief. There is no need of a miracle; he sends relief in the ordinary way by reminding some friend that a cloak is needed. He who took notice

of the 'vesture and garments' (*Psa.* 22:18) of the Head, is the same who here takes notice of the 'cloak' of one of the members.

2. *God's Love to Souls Is Independent of External Circumstances.* Here is a beloved saint, a man of God honoured and gifted above most, one whom God once caught up for a season (like Moses on the mount) to the third heaven; and yet this man has no wealth, no ample resources at command. Nay, he is really poor; he cannot buy a cloak in Rome, his funds are so low; he must wait till he gets the one he left at Troas. See how the Lord may be intensely loving those who are in poverty and discomfort, and who are friendless and destitute. He may see it best to leave his children in want of all earthly things; but he will not love them the less on that account. 'Know ye not that God has chosen the poor of this world, rich in faith, and heirs of the kingdom which he hath promised to those that love him?' (*James* 2:5). Here is one before us in want of a cloak to cover his shivering body, who nevertheless shall appear with Christ clothed with his house from heaven.

3. *An Example of Patience.* The winter was now near (verse 21); the snow would soon be covering Soracte and other hills round Rome. He had no friends at hand to come forward on his behalf; only Luke was with him, a brother as destitute of means as himself. Perhaps, too, he wished to act on the principle 'It is more blessed to give than to receive', and was unwilling to apply to anyone for help. He was in the Mamertine prison of Rome, solitary for the most part, and tried by the sad thought that his Christian friends in the city were acting, for the time, the part of the disciples at the cross, forsaking and fleeing from one in peril. It seems too, his 'books' had been forgotten along with his cloak, as if by this forgetfulness, the Lord wished to add to the trials of his servant, and to teach us that, great Apostle as Paul was, he was yet after all as liable to infirmities as any of us. Under all this, nevertheless, Paul is happy, patient, content; nay, looking upward, his face glows with delight,

and he exclaims: 'Henceforth there is laid up for me a crown of righteousness, which the Lord, the righteous Judge, shall give to me at that day; and not to me only, but unto all them also that love his appearing'! (verse 8).

4. *The Secret of Peace and Joy.* If Paul is happy, if Paul can sing for joy, it is not because he has external advantages and comforts. For he is in a gloomy prison; Roman guards pace in front of his cell; chains are on his hands; and he has no other than prison-fare; he cannot even keep himself warm, for his one cloak has been forgotten. What is it then that makes him so joyful? What is the secret of his peace and contentment? He tells it in this same letter (1:12). 'I am not ashamed; for I know whom I have believed; and am persuaded that he is able to keep that which I have committed to him against that day.' His eye and heart were on Christ's Cross, the ground of acceptance, and on Christ's Crown as his reward. He found God reconciled to him, a sinner, not because of personal merit, or attainment, or services, or past privileges, or prayers, but simply because of the Lord Jesus, 'WHOM (said he) I HAVE BELIEVED'. He trusted that same Jesus whom he believed to keep for him all he had committed to him till the great day of his return in glory, the day when he was to receive his crown (4:8). O ye poor, have you less in your home than Paul had in his prison? Yet you see, wants did not hinder his rapturous delight in him whom his soul had found to be hid treasure. Stand, if it must be so, on the bare floor and within empty walls; Paul did the same, and yet was as happy as when he came down from the third heavens. It was all because his soul had found the Righteous One as all his salvation! This was the secret of all his peace and joy—Christ believed in, for present acceptance; Christ expected, for future glory. And fail not to notice the emphasis placed on 'Righteousness' and 'Righteous' (4:8); for these terms tell how solid was the foundation of his hopes. The Judge, the righteous Judge,

the Judge who dispenses crowns of righteousness only, will on that day be able to assign such a crown to Paul, 'the chief of sinners'; because Paul has believed on him who is the Righteous One, and so has become one with him.

5. *A Lesson as to the Use of Means.* When now, last of all, we advert to the *'books and the parchments'*, we may find some further instruction. We see how even an inspired apostle, who had been in a third heaven, thought himself not to have attained all that he could learn here. He did not throw aside the help of other men's labours; he wished to have 'books' beside him to study. I scarcely think that by these were meant 'the Scriptures'; for I do not think Paul would fail to keep these beside him. True, he might by an oversight leave his Bible behind him, at Troas, as well as his cloak; but this is not very probable. At any rate, see how this man of God goes on reading and studying the things of God, till the day of his death. Here is humility; and here is direction to us as to the course we must take if we would grow in grace to the end. We must not forget our 'books': minister and people must be as Paul, 'meditating on the law of God day and night', and so be as 'a tree planted by rivers of water, whose leaf never withers' (*Psa.* 1:3).

As to the 'parchments'. They may have been documents by which he wished to prove his Roman citizenship, though others suppose they were documents regarding his personal effects, which he wished to arrange before his death: or they may have been simply some valuable writings. The lesson for us is, that saints must go on using common means, so long as we are here. While the eye of the happy believer is directed upward to him whom he believes, and who brings him the crown of righteousness, and while no poverty, no cold, no privation, no loneliness, interferes with this look of faith and hope, the means put within our reach are never to be despised. The 'books' and the 'parchments' must be sent for. And if this hold good of such helps, then not less emphatically may we press the use of other helps, such as the ordinances of Public Worship. 'Forsake not the assembling of yourselves together, as the manner of some is; but exhort one another; and so much the more as ye see THE DAY approaching' (*Heb.* 10:25).

16

'A LITTLE WINE'

Drink no longer water, but use a little wine
for thy stomach's sake and thine often infirmities.
1 Timothy 5:23

All Scripture is given by inspiration of God, and is profitable'
(*2 Tim.* 3:16). God is the author of all Scripture to this extent,
that he has intimated to us that he is for every sentence in the
Written Word. Every clause there has been inserted by him for a
special purpose.

Quite true, there are some portions that are apt to offend a
superficial reader, and some that seem at first sight barren and
unmeaning. But even in this the Word is like God its author; for
in his *Providence*, he does many things that offend; and on the
face of *Creation* has left not a few spaces that seem very useless at
the best. When, however, all these are carefully examined, we are
not long of having our first impressions changed. We find there is
something very precious below the surface.

The text in 1 Timothy 5:23 (like that other, *2 Tim.* 4:13) is one of
the kind in question, '*Drink no longer water, but use a little wine for*
thy stomach's sake, and thy frequent infirmities.' Let me show that in
reality it contains things of great value, every way worthy of the
Holy Ghost.

1. It bears upon our being *'faithful in the least'*. Our Lord has
taught his disciples to be conscientiously careful and circumspect in

smaller matters, as well as greater (*Luke* 16:10). And in accordance with this teaching, Timothy was led to consult Paul upon a point of comparatively small importance, but yet one that proved his scrupulous anxiety to please his Lord in all things, and do nothing wherein he could not look for the Divine blessing. It was a matter about his health of body, his 'stomach', and 'frequent infirmities'. In reply to this part of his letter, Paul wrote the verse before us. And it is worthwhile noticing that in replying he did not treat Timothy's question about health as one that might be passed over and disregarded. No; after speaking about very weighty matters, such as 'the mystery of godliness', 'apostatizing from the faith', 'the conduct of office-bearers', 'the exercise of discipline', he proceeds with the same care to attend to Timothy's personal inquiry.[1] Paul knew (for the Holy Ghost knew) the connection that exists between a right state of health and the proper discharge of duty in our office. He wished it to be always remembered, that attention to our physical state is necessary to the right performance of duty. The Lord might have made our souls independent of the body, but he has not so arranged. Are you a minister? Are you a teacher? You cannot do justice to yourself or to those under your care, if you are careless about your bodily state, indifferent to exercise, to food, to sleep, to good air, to anything conducive to a right state of health.

2. It bears upon *the use of medicine*. Timothy is directed to use special means. He is not told to leave all to take its course and just go on with his work. The Holy Ghost by Paul inculcates in many ways the doctrine of divine sovereignty, but nowhere for a moment countenances fatalism. He enjoins the use of means; he holds us responsible for the use of means. Hence, no doubt, even in working the miraculous cure of Hezekiah, there was application of means

---

[1] As in *1 Cor.* 15, and then 16:1-2, the Holy Spirit guides him to pass on at once from the doctrine of the Glorious Resurrection of the Just to the practical subject of a Collection for the poor saints.

at the same time: 'Let him take a lump of figs and lay it for a plaster upon the boil, and he shall recover' (*Isa.* 38:21). It is fatalism, not faith, to set aside skilful physicians. The sixth commandment comes in here in full force, enjoining the use of all right remedies. At the same time, be not as Asa, in the day of his trouble (*2 Chron.* 16:12), when he overlooked the Lord, while he assiduously sought the help of physicians. The 'disease in his foot' was 'exceeding great'; it grew worse and worse till he died: not however because he sought the help of medical skill, but because he did not acknowledge the Lord 'who healeth all our diseases' (*Psa.* 103:3).

3. It bears on *the subject of miracles.* It casts a side-light on that point, which is very interesting. Paul, who so often wrought miracles: who, formerly, at Ephesus, where Timothy then resided, so healed disease that the very touch of a handkerchief from his person chased the disease away (*Acts* 19:12), and made evil spirits flee, does not propose to work a miracle in behalf of Timothy. Nor is it likely that Timothy asked this; for he knew very well that when Epaphroditus, a most useful pastor at Philippi, was ill, Paul wrought no miracle to raise him up. Just as afterwards, when another friend and brother was sick, Trophimus, nothing was done for him beyond the use of ordinary means which in the course of some weeks might bring a cure (*2 Tim.* 4:20).

We find that John, the beloved disciple, acted in no other manner in the case of Gaius (*3 John* 2); working no miracle in his behalf. And why all this? To teach us some weighty truths. 1. The gift of miracles was for the glory of God, not the honour of men. No apostle could work a miracle unless God plainly indicated to him that he desired it to be done on that person. 2. The apostles did not act to gratify self; they had supreme regard to the will of God. 3. The Lord did not then, nor does he now, wish his ministers and workers to be free from weaknesses, and infirmities and trials. That earthen vessel, not very attractive, and always ready to break in pieces, is very often the vessel in which he is pleased to put his treasure. He may use a strong, healthy, vigorous Paul, who can go on preaching as before after being stoned, after being five times beaten with rods, and three times made to bleed under the lash, and three times shipwrecked; but he wishes us to know, for the comfort of those whose frame is feeble, that he can and does use, in a remarkable way, such workmen as Timothy who groan under frequent infirmities. Richard Baxter, I suppose, often rejoiced in reading this verse that tells of Timothy's 'stomach' and sicknesses, and how he was left to struggle on against them in the use of ordinary means, such as *'a little wine'*.

4. It bears on the question of *Temperance and Total Abstinence*. Read the words again attentively. *'Use no longer water';* be no longer a mere water-drinker, *but use 'a little wine';* use wine; a little of it. We learn from this that there is *no sin in using wine*. It is here recommended for medicinal purposes; and if Timothy had not used it when he was thus enjoined, it would have been a sinful neglect. There is nothing sinful in the use of wine in itself; it is the manner and measure of using it that may be sinful; for as Proverbs 20:1 has warned us, 'Wine is a mocker'; it so often and so insidiously leads on to evil. But Christ at the marriage in Cana gave it for good ends. There was a blessing in it as used there. And so, when Timothy used it for medicine, there was blessing in it.

But, at the same time, we learn from this very text, that there may be good and solid reasons for *altogether abstaining from wine*.[1] Paul knew that Timothy had hitherto abstained entirely, and he does not blame him in the slightest degree. Nay, the tone of his words is all the other way; only, he tells that now it will be right for him to deviate a little from his former practice. What Timothy's

[1] The Nazarites and Rechabites rigidly abstained from even taking a grape: but this was not because there is sin in that fruit. They had special reasons, and good reasons, for abstaining; but the sinfulness of using wine, in any circumstances, was not one.

reasons were for abstaining up till now, we cannot tell; but he had seen good cause in Ephesus for being an abstainer. And any man among us who knows that £147,000,000 are spent in strong drink every year in Great Britain, and that there are not less than about 99,000 public houses, as well as about 39,000 beer shops, may well stand still and consider if he should not shun the very appearance of giving countenance to this enormous evil. Indeed, does not our passage justify us in inferring that *there ought to be some special reason* for anyone *indulging* in the use of wine? Do it (says Paul, or rather the Holy Ghost by Paul) 'for *thy stomach's sake* and thy frequent infirmities'. And even then, use only *'a little'*. No doubt, Paul understood his patient's case; and certainly he wished him to be cautious even in taking a little. Not like many of our physicians who, without knowing the habits or the constitutional tendencies of the sick one, give advice that is understood to allow the free use of wine. And all the more should we be nervously cautious here since everyone knows that our wines are far more dangerous than the strongest wines of those days. The alcohol in our wines is what recommends them to most; in old days, it was the nourishment they yielded.

5. Take a parting look at Timothy. Do you feel inclined to say of him, 'I suspect he must have been one who was over scrupulous, who brought himself into bondage by his tenderness of conscience. Only think of him consulting the great apostle about this trifling matter regarding himself.' We reply: there is another way of looking at this man of God. He acted thus because he sought to do as we are enjoined in 1 Corinthians 10:31, 'Whether ye eat or drink, do all to the glory of God.' In him we see a fine manifestation of 'the heart of flesh' (*Ezek.* 36:26), the tender conscience, that gives good heed to every hint and intimation of the Divine will, and is guided in every decision not by a regard to self but by a reference to his pleasure. This is true holiness of heart; and in all holiness there is

not bondage, but perfect liberty and gladness.

6. Look once more at our God and Saviour. In this text, we see him, through his servant Paul, attending minutely to the concerns of young Timothy. What a heart of love. 'The very hairs of your head are all numbered', says he to us (*Matt.* 10:30). 'There shall not an hair of your head perish' (*Luke* 21:18).

Thanks be to our Prophet Jesus, for this verse about Timothy and the 'little wine'!

———————

Some other books by Andrew Bonar
published by the Trust

The Visitor's Book of Texts

Paperback, 296 pp.

ISBN: 978 1 84871 071 9

A useful aid for pastoral visitation.

Heavenly Springs

Paperback, 244 pp.

ISBN: 978 0 85151 479 6

Meditations for each Lord's day of the year.

Robert Murray M'Cheyne

Paperback, 192 pp.

ISBN: 978 0 85151 085 9

One of the greatest Christian biographies ever written—a true classic.

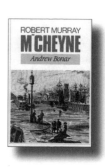